RETURN OF THE

RETURN OF THE WOLF

SUCCESSES AND THREATS IN THE US AND CANADA

STEVE GROOMS

How to order: single copies may be ordered online at www.novavistapub.com.
In North America, you may phone 503-590-8898. Elsewhere, dial +32-14-21-11-21.

The author gratefully acknowledges permission by Rocky Barker to draw heavily upon his story about Wolf B2. The original story by Barker, "The Story of the Wolf That Changed Idaho," appeared in the May 9, 2004 edition of the *Idaho Statesman*.

Photo Credits

The copyright of each photograph in this book belongs to the photographer, except for the image of Aldo Leopold. No reproduction of the photographic images contained herein may be made without the express permission of the copyright holder.

Unless noted below, all photos in *Return of the Wolf* and the cover photos are by Michael H. Francis (see page 157).

Page 21: Aldo Leopold examining specimens in his lab, 1938. Photo by Robert Octking, Courtesy of the Aldo Leopold Foundation Archives
Page 70, upper left: US Fish & Wildlife Service
Page 70, lower right and page 72: Melissa McGaw
Page 93: Carissa Knaack
Page 104: L. Dave Mech
Pages 112-13, 117, 118, 121: Wendy Shattil/Bob Rozinski
Page 143: John and Mary Theberge
Page 146: Photo of Sophie Haley by Steve Grooms

ISBN 90-77256-08-3

D/2005/9797/1

Printed and bound in Singapore

20 19 18 17 16 15 14 13 12 11 10 9 8 7 6 5 4 3 2

Editorial development: Andrew Karre
Cover design: Astrid De Deyne
Text design: Layout Sticker

Contents

Foreword

On July 16, 2004, it was my privilege to give the keynote address at a press conference at the Wildlife Science Center, near Forest Lake, Minnesota. On that day, the United States Fish and Wildlife Service announced the decision to delist the gray wolf in the Eastern Distinct Population Segment – a monumental accomplishment.

When the wolf was listed as an endangered species in 1974, only 700 wolves were left in the Lower 48 states of the US. What happened in the next 30 years has been absolutely amazing. Wolves responded with their fabled resilience until the population of gray wolves in the recovery area is over 3,000 – twice the level managers hoped to reach – with an additional 850 or so in the northern Rockies.

What the wolves did might be less impressive than what humans have done. People have changed their minds about wolves, moving from fear and hate to wonder and appreciation.

The International Wolf Center has played its part in that historic change. Since 1985, we have done our best to teach the world the truth about this complicated, fascinating predator. In 1993 we opened our flagship building in Ely, Minnesota. The center includes a resident wolf pack, educational exhibits, and an array of adventure programs.

Now it is time to declare victory and return the wolf to normal wildlife management. The comeback of wolves is one of the most inspiring stories in management history.

On that bright, summer day, my eloquence apparently didn't impress the center's resident pack of wolves. As I was winding up for my conclusion, the center's resident pack of 53 wolves cut loose with a group howl that drowned me out. I had to wait for several minutes. When they let me go on, I concluded by quoting the final words of this book:

> The true measure of the morality of a political society is how justly it treats its least powerful and popular citizens. In much the same sense, the ecological decency of a society can be measured by how it treats the most troublesome and notorious animal species. For our society, that is the wolf.
>
> When North Americans prove they have learned to live with wolves, we can begin to like ourselves a little better. It will then be time to ponder how we can improve our relations with several hundred other species, but not before pausing to celebrate the extraordinary progress represented by the return of the wolf.

You have a wonderful experience ahead of you as you read the rest of Steve Grooms' story of the return of the wolf.

Walter F. Medwid, Executive Director, International Wolf Centerr

CHAPTER 1

The Wolves Are Returning

Wolves are returning.

They're coming home to lands where wolves have lived ever since the glaciers retreated but where no wolves have been seen for a long time – for years, for decades, for centuries.

Their return means different things to different people.

Close encounters

On an October night in 1992, Kathe Grooms is driving northeast on Highway 13, headed for our family cabin along the shores of Lake Superior. Molly, our teenage daughter, sits beside Kathe and chatters to keep her awake. It is dark, and a motorist always has to worry about whacking a deer along here.

Near the mouth of the Brule River, the car sweeps through a bend and is mounting a little rise when two large animals appear in the headlights. They halt and swing majestic heads toward the onrushing car.

"Deer, Molly! No. What are those . . . dogs?" Kathe knows there are no houses anywhere near here. It makes no sense that dogs would be out running around here at night.

For a long moment, the animals do not move. Lit by the car's headlights, their eyes glow like Cyalume light sticks.

"WOLVES, Mom! They're WOLVES!"

The car is within twenty feet of the wolves when they dive off the asphalt and disappear in dog-hair aspen south of the highway.

Molly has adored wolves for years. Her bedroom is virtually a shrine to wolves. She has a collection of books about wolves – serious books, some written by biologists. Molly's dad would later borrow those books to do research when he wrote this book. Wolf researcher L. Dave Mech is a personal hero of Molly's. She sleeps each night under the watchful eyes of twenty-eight wolves in photos on her bedroom walls.

Molly knows how improbable this wolf sighting is. At the time, Wisconsin researchers could only document the presence of a few dozen wolves in the state, and she has just seen two of them. Tears of joy well up in Molly's eyes.

Some of the wolves now repopulating former wolf country wear collars that emit signals that can be detected by biologists who wander should be, and what regulations should be enacted to manage them. And when all the "stakeholders" and experts have had their fights, they hire lawyers to wage the same fight all over in a court of law. Ultimately, some judge who might have gotten a C in the only biology class he ever took might be obliged to make a ruling that actually determines the course of wolf management.

Early in the Yellowstone wolf-restoration project, federal trappers hear a wolf has left the park and seems to be headed for Canada, where she was born, taking her pups with her. Because she wears a collar, she is easy to follow. When she kills some sheep, the trappers swoop in and surround the carcass with traps. They don't want any more livestock attacks to generate negative publicity for the program.

Since the mother wolf's radio signal indicates she has moved on, the trappers decide they don't need to check their traps every few hours as they usually would do. They don't know that one pup has split off the pack to return to that tasty sheep carcass. They don't know that the pup has placed a front paw on the pan of a big trap set for its mother.

The trappers have been shadowed by an animal rights group. They find the pup shortly after it gets caught. They do not, however, inform authorities. Instead, they camp on the site with cameras for thirty-six hours to film the pup's struggles. When the trappers finally return, the pup's leg has been deprived of blood for so long it will have to be amputated.

That wolf – perhaps the most beautiful wolf I've seen – was moved to the Wildlife Science Center, a research and educational facility located near Forest Lake, Minnesota. Although the Yellowstone wolf could not talk, he taught youngsters and other visitors some lessons about people's complicated attitudes toward animals, especially wolves.

The debates

At one time, the topic surest to set people arguing was religion. Today, if you want to start

No animal matches the ability of wolves to stir controversy. People fight about wolves.

a fight with someone, say something about wolves. I recently heard a radio commentator say the first fight started when Adam barked at Eve for eating the apple. I know better. The first argument started earlier than that, when both were still living in the Garden of Eden. Adam made a careless comment, admitting to Eve that he had been trapping wolves because they had been eating too many of his deer.

"YOUR deer?" howled Eve. "YOUR deer? Oh, that is SO like a man!"

The first argument in history was about wolf management. No doubt about it!

At a meeting to discuss wolf management, an old couple who live in a small town in north-central Minnesota show up to display photos of their golden retriever. The dog was killed by wolves that entered its yard, and the photos are not pretty. It had never occurred to the old couple that their canine partner was in any threat as it slept on the back porch.

A woman representing a pro-wolf group is not sympathetic. She tells the old couple, "That was your fault, you know. You had no business letting a dog out unsupervised in wolf country."

The old couple is confused. How did it happen that their small town became "wolf country?" And how did they become irresponsible pet owners just for letting their old friend doze in the sunlight in his own backyard?

The Druid Pack drama

When wolves were released into Yellowstone in 1995 and 1996, managers talked hopefully about the day when park visitors might hear the chesty bawl of wolves echoing across the wilderness. Visitors wouldn't see wolves, of course, but they'd know they were there.

The wolves had some surprises in store for the experts. They flourished as expected, and yet in almost every other regard they astonished biologists by not doing things wolves "always" do and by doing many things wolves "never" do.

The first surprise was how visible Yellowstone's new arrivals became. In particular, the pack that claimed territory in the Lamar Valley in the northern end of Yellowstone Park began living their lives in plain view of tourists and managers. The Druid Peak Pack was named for a nearby mountain. Soon everyone was talking about "the Druids" as if they were celebrities.

The Druids seemed to sense that people were no threat. A road running by the valley gives humans easy access to the area. The open terrain allows anyone with a spotting scope to observe wolves killing elk and playing with each other. Never has it been so easy for humans to observe wild wolves.

Yellowstone's wolves began drawing visitors from all over the world. The Druids became the most studied wolf pack in history. Movie crews began grinding film through their cameras, taking advantage of the unanticipated cooperation of the Druids. Among them was filmmaker Bob Landis, who produced two films based on eight years of filming in Yellowstone. His "Wolves – A Legend Returns to Yellowstone" might be the most fascinating and authentic film ever made about wolves.

Some of the power of that film comes from the soap-opera lives of the three wolves known to managers as Wolves 21, 40, and 42. Wolf 21 was the Druids' alpha male, and 40 was their alpha female. Wolf 42 was her sister.

It is an amazing story. While astonished researchers and cameramen recorded their lives, these three wolves played out a drama of Shakespearian grandeur. Wolf 40, the alpha female, was a harsh queen who dominated her subordinates with gratuitous violence. After driving her mother and other sister out of the pack, 40 focused her aggression on her sister, 42. For obvious reasons, the film crew nicknamed the beleaguered sister "Cinderella."

The alpha male, Wolf 21, mated with both 40 and Cinderella, although normally an alpha male will only mate with the alpha female. Both Druid females bore litters of 21's pups. When Cinderella's pups disappeared, researchers suspected 40 of killing them. They didn't see it happen, but the guess was consistent with her style.

A year later, the two Druid sisters each had pups again. Once more, 40 apparently tried to kill Cinderella's pups. This time, Cinderella fought back ferociously. She inflicted mortal wounds on her aggressive sister. Cinderella might have been aided by other pack members in the first recorded act of regicide among wolves.

After 40's demise, Cinderella moved her seven pups to 40's den and formed a combined litter. She successfully mothered all of them. Wolf 21 accepted Cinderella as his mate, and over the years, he endeared himself to observers by showering her and their pups with affection. The duo (nicknamed the "Hollywood wolves" because they were film stars) aged gracefully over the years, turning an attractive shade of silver.

Cinderella was killed early in 2003. No humans observed the event, but all evidence suggests she died after being attacked by wolves from Mollie's Pack, the arch-enemies of the Druids. At the age of eight, she was old for a wolf in the wild. When a crowd of Yellowstone wolf watchers heard the old queen was dead, several broke down in tears.

They weren't alone. After Cinderella died, Wolf 21 sat moaning for days. In the words of Doug Smith, the head of the Yellowstone Wolf Project, "[He] howled his guts out. People say they heard him howl more since she died than he did in the five years before that."

Was 21 mourning?

"I can't say that wolves mourn," said Smith, "I'm a scientist and that's not a scientific thing to say. But I do know he acted differently than he ever did before. You can draw your own conclusions."

A second chance

All this time, wolves continue to come home, home to habitat where wolves flourished for centuries before the great extirpation. Many move at night, filtering through moonlit brush as silently as smoke. As they trot over old trails that haven't seen a wolf in many decades, they pass many places where ancient wolves were trapped, shot, or poisoned. But these wolves aren't interested in ghosts. The real threats to them lie in the present, not the past.

It is hazardous for a wolf to leave the relative safety of its own pack and its own territory. If it blunders into territory defended by other wolves, it might die in a frenzy of snapping teeth. If it crosses a highway, it might be struck by a rushing UPS truck. If it stands in view of a human with a rifle who is nursing a grudge against authority, the dispersing wolf could be shot. Sometimes a dispersing wolf breeds successfully only to watch the pups sicken and die of diseases against which evolution has given

wolves no protection.

And yet some survive. And then some of their offspring survive.

For some people, the return of wolves brings humans a precious gift: the gift of a second chance. Some people want to believe that our society is now a little wiser and more tolerant than our long, ugly history of wolf hatred indicates.

Some people have high hopes for the return of the wolf. They know things won't be perfect. Somewhere, a wolf will slash through a bawling mass of sheep like a chainsaw. Somewhere, an embittered man will kill a wolf and attach its radio collar to a log he throws in a river, just to spite the researchers. It isn't all pretty.

Nevertheless, the return of the wolf seems a momentous turning point. As wolves return and people accept them, something new is happening between humans and North America's most controversial predator.

We have been given a second chance.

Surely, things will go better this time than they did the first time around.

A young couple living in the wilderness of northeastern Minnesota is roused from bed one night by an insistent knocking. Who could be calling at this improbable hour?

The knocker turns out to be a wolf with a radio collar and badly diseased lungs. After initial alarm, the couple brings the wolf into the cabin, placing him near the warmth of the wood stove. He does not struggle.

Throughout the night, the wolf accepts their care as if this kindness is what he expected, what he came for. Ultimately, compassion is not enough to remove the infected soup filling his lungs. In the profound darkness of predawn, his breathing grows labored. Just at sunrise, he dies in their arms.

The return of the wolf means many things. To some people, it represents a precious second chance.

CHAPTER 2

Wolves and Humans

The wolf was once a great ecological success story. Wolves hunted all of Eurasia and the New World, from sun-baked Mexico to the frozen Arctic. Wolves were omnipresent in the northern hemisphere except in the most arid deserts and highest mountain peaks. Wherever they lived, wolves were the top predators, feeding on large, hoofed animals. Today, wolves have been eliminated from a large percentage of their historic range, both in North America and throughout the world. Some populations hang on in isolated remnant groups. Wolves have not been seen for centuries in many places where they formerly thrived. Perhaps no other species' numbers have fallen so low in so much of its former range after thriving in a wide variety of habitats.

The widespread collapse of wolf populations is all the more surprising when one considers the wolf's remarkable physical abilities, social structure, and adaptability. Most endangered species become endangered because they are too narrowly adapted or sluggish to respond to change. The wolf could not be more different. No delicate specialist, the wolf is one of the toughest, smartest, and most flexible mammalian predators in evolutionary history. It should have been one of evolution's great winners, not a species flirting with extinction in so many regions of the world.

There is no dispute about how this improbable collapse happened. Wolves have declined through no inherent weakness, but because they have suffered ferocious persecution by humans. Worldwide, no other species has been singled out for such systematic extermination. In North America, the early 20th century saw a concerted effort to eradicate wolves as if they were a scourge that could not be tolerated.

Of course, humans have persecuted other animal species. People have traditionally killed venomous snakes on sight. Yet there is something uniquely nasty about the way humans have treated wolves. The wolf holds the wretched distinction of being the most misunderstood and persecuted animal in western civilization. People have called wolves murderous, treacherous, gluttonous, savage, and cowardly. As if that weren't bad enough, wolves have been damned from church pulpits as sulphur-breathing minions of the devil himself. Humans have hated wolves with a nearly hysterical passion.

Why?

Who's afraid of the big bad wolf?

It has become a cliché to blame wolf hatred on European fairy tales. After all, it was a wolf that threatened to "blow the house in" on three little pigs. It was a wolf that swallowed the feckless duck in "Peter and the Wolf." Above all, in a tale some scholars believe has dark sexual undertones, it was a wolf that gobbled Granny and seduced Little Red Riding Hood. That story alone might have provoked the deaths of many thousands of wolves.

But blaming old fairy tales doesn't explain much about our history of wolf hatred. It begs the question of why wolves and not other large predators were singled out as symbols of evil. And it grants too much influence to a handful of fables. No, the true origins of wolf hatred lie elsewhere.

Obviously, wolves have suffered because people feared them. Very few northern hemisphere animals are capable of killing humans. While biologists today tell us wolves pose no significant threat to people, that's an extremely modern notion.

North American settlers were less frightened by fairy tales than by all the presumably authentic stories they read and heard about wolves attacking people. For some reason, Russia and France exported more than their share of such stories. A typical example is the Robert Browning poem "Ivan Ivanovitch," in which a wolf pack pursues a sleigh across a wintry Russian landscape. To save their own lives, the cowardly men chucked children out of the sleigh to distract the wolves. If such stories seem comically macabre today, they were viewed as gospel truth by earlier North American settlers.

Today's admirers of wolves cannot understand how people ever failed to appreciate the beauty of wolves. One answer lies in the way wolves were rendered by artists of earlier times. If an artist exaggerates certain feature – making the snout longer and thinner, the teeth more prominent, the eyes set closer together – a lovely animal appears menacing. If the wolf is depicted as gaunt and hungry, it is all the more threatening.

By contrast, most people today visualize wolves as they appear in recent photographs and paintings. The models for these works are captive wolves that, while not quite chubby, are fed well and look it. The wolves we see are noble, friendly, and intelligent. They look more like pets than slavering demons of the night. Most wild wolves I've seen are thinner and spookier than the sleek, glossy wolves that populate today's coffee-table wolf books. Wildlife photographers sometimes complain that editors will not buy their pictures of wild wolves, as they don't fit the modern notion of what a wolf looks like. Wild wolves, lean and shaggy, don't fit a stereotype that has been created by photographs of captive-raised wolves that are placed briefly in wild settings to have their picture taken.

A friend who used to deliver mail around a wilderness lake using a dog team was once chased for several miles by a wolf pack. Even though Charlotte knew the wolves were responding to the fact her lead bitch was in heat, she was unnerved by the experience. A day after the chase, she bought a snowmobile. Snow machines have their failings, but they do not go into estrus and they do not attract wolves. She had been scared.

All in all, it is too easy today for us to ridicule such fears. Terrified farm families living on the frontier spent fitful nights while wolves moaned lugubriously from nearby timber. Those people "knew" that wolves would seize any chance to kill a human. They feared wolves in ways that are impossible for us to appreciate. We shouldn't be too quick to scoff at them for being ignorant.

And yet it is difficult to rationalize the continued hatred for wolves. Mountain lions have killed several humans recently, including joggers, mountain bikers, and children. Grizzly

The difference between the romantic image of the wolf and reality can hardly be overstated.

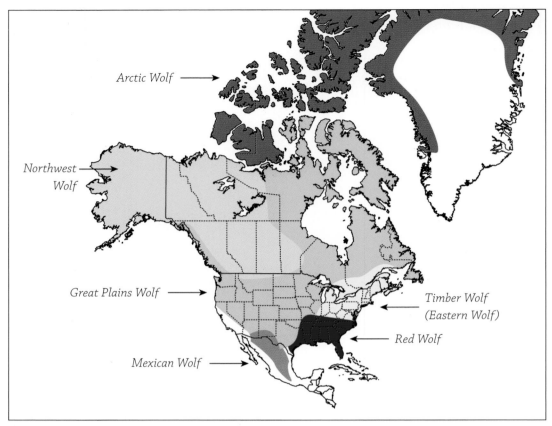

Possible original ranges of red wolf and gray wolf subtypes in North America.

bears kill humans. Any large predator is a potential threat to humans, so it seems strange that wolves continue to excite so much passion when other animals are demonstrably more dangerous.

The hound from hell

Christianity has fostered wolf hatred. The few references to wolves in the Bible are not complimentary. A central metaphor depicts Jesus as the shepherd who cares for his flock of believers. The image of Christians as sheep is hardly flattering, especially to anyone who knows sheep. But the real loser in this metaphor is the wolf. If Christians are sheep, wolves (since they prey on sheep) are murderers and possibly agents of the devil.

Wolves acquired all sorts of demonic significance in the tortured imaginations of medieval Europeans. Priests proclaimed that wolves were Satan's minions. A 15th-century council of theologians studied the best research on the matter and announced that werewolves unquestionably existed. As a consequence, several men were burned at the stake or buried alive after confessing to murders committed while they were in werewolf form. A young man named Jean Grenier made a similar confession, although his death sentence was commuted. Grenier spent his final years in a friary, running about on all fours, eating rotten meat, and believing himself to be a wolf. It was so common for demented people to believe they were wolves that a name, *lycanthropy*, was coined to identify this delusion.

Wolves somehow became associated with all the carnal appetites the church wanted to suppress. Incongruously, wolves – although they are lucky indeed if they experience sex once a year – were excoriated for being promiscuous.

The beast of waste and destruction

When European settlers began carving villages from the wilderness of North America, wolves became symbols of chaos and economic waste. Priests and preachers in the 1600s urged their congregations to make a "fruitful field" out of the "howling wilderness." The howl of the wilderness was supplied, it went without saying, by the wolf. Wolves were associated with all the godless wastelands that had yet to be tamed and put into productive fields, in the settler's minds.

The Europeans who settled North America believed that mankind should hold dominion over all lesser animals. Animals were considered valuable to the extent that they served man's needs. From such a utilitarian perspective, wolves were less than useless. They lacked intrinsic value. Worse, they destroyed valuable livestock and wildlife. To this day, wolf supporters are sometimes taunted by wolf haters demanding to know, "What *good* is a wolf?"

Both wolves and Native Americans were reviled as impediments to Manifest Destiny, the inevitable expansion of Euro-centric culture from the Atlantic to the Pacific. Even those eccentric folks who admired Indians or wolves assumed they had to be eliminated because nothing could be permitted to halt the march of "progress." To that end, both Indians and wolves were persecuted, sometimes by having a bounty put on them to encourage their destruction.

When much of the West became sectioned off into livestock ranches, wolf hatred soared to heights that seem barbaric even in the context of an already horrific history of wolf hatred. Not content to kill wolves, people began inventing ways to kill them painfully.

Cattlemen laced carrion with ground glass, leaving it for wolves. Wolves caught in leg-hold traps were released with their jaws wired shut so they would die slowly. Wolves were set ablaze. There was something profoundly personal and ugly about the way people hated wolves.

The growing popularity of sport hunting in the 19th century provided yet another rationale for destroying wolves. Hunters believed that wolves would wipe out herds of game animals, diminishing their own sport. They urged managers to kill wolves in order to encourage strong game populations. "Wolf control" was a popular game management concept because it promised to create abundant game populations without requiring hunters to exercise any restraint by restricting their own harvest.

One of the most enthusiastic wolf control agents in the 1930s was a young biologist named Aldo Leopold. Leopold believed eliminating wolves would protect livestock and restore badly depleted stocks of elk, deer, moose, and other game animals in the West.

At the top of the food chain

While it is easy – too easy – to dismiss Little Red Riding Hood as a silly fable, debunking fairy tales doesn't help us understand the most fundamental and potent motivation for wolf hatred: competition (or you could call it greed). Humans hate wolves because wolves eat the stuff we like to eat. Or, if you are a livestock

Aldo Leopold was pivotal in changing attitudes about wolves.

producer, wolves eat the cattle or sheep you count on selling to make a living.

Large ungulates – hoofed, deerlike animals – are the natural prey of wolves. Wild and domesticated ungulates also happen to be the food most prized by humans. Whenever wolves kill a moose or elk, humans think, "Hey! That's one less for us!" When wolves kill a sheep, the loss to the shepherd is both emotional and financial.

This natural competition has resulted in a sorry pattern that has been repeated endlessly throughout the history of European expansion in the New World. First, settlers deplete the wild ungulates that are the natural prey for wolves. They often then alter the habitat so it can no longer support wild ungulates. Then they fill the empty habitat with livestock. When wolves prey on the only remaining food source, those domesticated ungulates, people retaliate with vengeance.

Wolves and humans are two predators perched uncomfortably near each other at the top of the food chain. More accurately, what we call the food chain is a fat pyramid. The great broad base of the pyramid is vegetation. The smaller midsection contains prey animals, such as rabbits and deer. The sharp peak of the pyramid is composed of predators. One of the maxims of ecology is that food pyramids can support only a limited number of predators. A corollary is that predators don't cheerfully share a limited prey base. They compete, sometimes violently.

I earlier described wolves as the top predator of large mammals, but that isn't strictly true. Humans are actually the top predator of large mammals such as ungulates. Humans and wolves are doomed to be direct competitors for a limited food supply.

A striking characteristic of wolves is the great affection they show for each other.

Wolf hatred as self-hatred

Even after considering the many reasons humans fear or resent wolves, it is difficult to account for the virulence of wolf hatred. Ultimately, it seems that wolves have suffered because they remind humans too much of themselves. Wolves are, after all, the most intelligent and social wild animal in the northern hemisphere. They are like us in many ways.

This theme has been developed in convincing detail by the writer Barry Lopez in his seminal book, *Of Wolves and Men*. Through the centuries, Lopez argues, we have projected onto wolves all the qualities we most despise or fear in ourselves. Wolves have not only been misperceived but also demonized in a virtual paroxysm of self-loathing. Over and over, the wolf we have persecuted is not the actual wolf that has fleas and hunts and howls in lonely places, but a conceptual wolf – a spooky, imagined wolf – that we have invented somewhere in the nether regions of our own psyches.

The new possibility

Three or four decades ago, the story of humans and wolves would have fit that unhappy description. But something has happened to alter the old antagonistic relationship, something so dramatically new that it is about as difficult to comprehend as the old tradition of wolf hatred.

No single person has influenced American attitudes toward wildlife more fundamentally than Aldo Leopold, so it is fitting that an incident in Leopold's life marks the start of a new perception of wolves. Leopold and some companions were riding in the White Mountains of New Mexico when they saw a wolf swim a river. She was met on the far side by six large pups. They wriggled joyously to celebrate her return. The men's response was as reflexive as swatting a mosquito: they blazed away with rifles. When they took stock of the outcome of their fusillade, the mother lay bleeding to death by the river's edge and one pup was dragging itself into the rocks.

And something astonishing happened. Looking into the eyes of the dying she-wolf, Leopold's sense of triumph changed to remorse.

> We reached the old wolf in time to watch a fierce green fire dying in her eyes. I realized then, and have known ever since, that there was something new to me in those eyes – something known only to her and to the mountain. I was young then, and full of trigger-itch; I thought that because fewer wolves meant more deer, that no wolves would mean hunters' paradise. But after seeing the green fire die, I sensed that neither the wolf nor the mountain would agree with such a view.

In that remarkable moment, centuries of wolf hatred collided with the basic decency and growing ecological wisdom of a single man . . . and the great shift from wolf hatred to wolf admiration became possible. It wouldn't happen soon – not even for Leopold, who continued to advocate wolf control for some time – but a new understanding of wolves was now a possibility.

What happened next was that a new discipline of wildlife research and wildlife management was founded, with Leopold himself being the central figure shaping this new science. In time, more and more of the people working with wolves approached their subject as scientists. A key innovation of the new science was that it accepted predators as equal partners in the ecological community, not "bad animals" that were bad because they killed other animals.

Adolph Murie established himself as a pioneer of wolf research when he undertook his study of wolves in Alaska's Mount McKinley Park (now Denali) in the 1940s. Murie had enough professionalism and integrity to see wolves as they were, not as he had been told they were. He described wolves as affectionate, cooperative animals that live in ecological balance with prey populations. But few people were paying attention.

A new climate of ecological awareness was being born three decades later when researcher L. David Mech published his book, *The Wolf*, in 1970. Mech wrote at a time when bounties had just been lifted from wolves in Minnesota. The general public paid wolves little attention, but hunters, game managers, and farmers opposed them. Although *The Wolf* was primarily addressed to scholars and students of wolves, Mech's intelligent and groundbreaking book became an unlikely crossover hit that sold to increasing legions of wolf fans. Mech, an energetic and multitalented man, continues to educate people about wolves with his work as a researcher, photographer, writer, manager, and as the founder of the International Wolf Center. More than any single person, he is responsible for fostering a new and more tolerant public perception of wolves.

Shortly after Mech's book appeared, the United States Congress passed the Endangered Species Act (ESA) of 1973. Wolves were among the first animals listed as endangered. That status brought wolves into the public eye and endowed them with a certain tragic, romantic identity they had never before enjoyed. The US's wolf policy made an astonishing about-face. Government wildlife managers began planning the restoration of wolves to habitat where governmental programs had just succeeded in eliminating them.

It is impossible to document the impact of countless wolf films airing on television, but beyond question they have been potent agents for change. Before Murie, virtually no human had actually seen wolves without looking through distorting veils of fear and myth. Now, that experience is routinely available to anyone tuning into wildlife shows on television.

In just a decade and a half, from 1970 to 1985, the wolf went from the scapegoat of the animal kingdom to one of its most revered citizens. Wolves have become the ultimate symbols of wilderness as well as the defining symbol of man's cruelty to animals. Artists who formerly paid the rent by cranking out waterfowl paintings began frequenting the wolf exhibits in zoos so they could produce credible paintings of the most popular subject for wildlife art. The Minnesota community of Ely, notorious in the 1970s as a bastion of wolf hatred, lobbied in the 1980s for the privilege of hosting an educational facility for the International Wolf Center. Mail-order businesses seem to be able to sell almost any product imaginable so long as it carries some image of a wolf. North Americans are falling in love with wolves.

Library bookshelves now groan under the weight of many revisionist, pro-wolf books, especially in juvenile fiction. In *The True Tale of the Three Little Pigs*, the author (A. Wolf) protests, "Hey, I was framed!" Children still might hear the story of Little Red Riding Hood, but they're more likely to be influenced by such books as Jean Craighead George's *Julie of the Wolves*. In that popular book, a girl is befriended by wolves. Youngsters now have a predominantly positive view of wolves.

Such a dramatic change, and all in a decade or two! How could this have happened? According to one juvenile literature library expert, today's kids are pro-wolf because today's books "present the scientific perspective on wolves."

Really? Are we witnessing the triumph of science over ignorance?

I don't think so. Consider Farley Mowat's *Never Cry Wolf*. Originally a book, it became a hit movie that lives on in television re-runs and video rentals. By presenting wolves as admirable and humans as vicious, *Never Cry Wolf* did for wolves what *Dances With Wolves* did for Native Americans: It turned an old negative stereotype on its head.

Never Cry Wolf must have presented unusual conflicts for wolf experts like Mech. The book was fiction that the author presented as nonfiction. In the act of scotching old myths,

People still have trouble seeing wolves as wolves, not as symbols of something else.

Mowat created new ones, such as the notion that wolves can live on a diet of mice. Yet in spite of its flaws and distortions, *Never Cry Wolf* was attractively written and sympathetic to wolves at a time when wolves needed every friend they could find.

Can a bad book be a good thing?

The three wolves

The anguished relationship between humans and wolves has thus taken another odd turn.

There are now three different wolves keeping uneasy company with one another in the North American imagination. The old demonic wolf lives on, especially in the minds of older, rural people. Their view is being rejected by rapidly growing numbers of wolf fans, many of whom adore wolves uncritically and regard them as inherently more noble than humans. Then there is the wolf of the biologist: a remarkable predator – neither demon nor saint – that has a peculiar ability to incite contentious management disputes. Unfortunately, the sober, factual image of the wolf is harder to promote than the other two, which are more appealing because they are inherently emotional.

Wolves were persecuted for centuries because they were reduced to symbols of evil. Now they are being worshipped by people who reduce them to symbols of wilderness and make them "poster children" for man's crimes against the natural world. People used to view wolves imperfectly through filters of greed and fear. They still do, but many also view wolves imperfectly through filters of guilt and romance.

After all this time, it remains almost as difficult as ever to see wolves not as symbols, but as wolves.

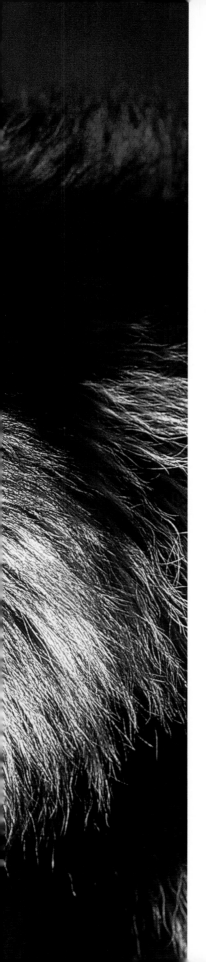

CHAPTER 3

Wolves of North America

All carnivores evolved from an ancient group of meat-eaters called *creodonts*. These otterlike creatures gave rise to two new types of carnivores. One was a catlike group that mostly lived in dense forests or jungles, practicing an ambush style of predation. The other was a doglike group that hunted more open terrain where sustained speed was critical. This group evolved long limbs to help them run down their prey.

In time, this second group produced the highly successful family we know as the *Canidae*, the doglike animals. It consists of several genera, the most prominent being the genus *Canis*. Included are the gray wolf, *Canis lupus*; the red wolf, *Canis rufus*; the domestic dog, *Canis familiaris*; the coyote, *Canis latrans*; several jackals; and Ruppell's fox.

The wolves of prehistory

Scientists have reconstructed the history of wolf evolution primarily through the painstaking and frustrating process of analyzing fossil evidence. Conclusions drawn from fossil evidence are now being confirmed or corrected by modern DNA studies. Combining all sources of information, we have a sense of how wolves developed.

According to some taxonomists, coyotes evolved from foxes some four or five million years ago. Between one and two million years ago, the coyote line split. One group consisted of a huskier version of today's coyote. The other group had more massive skulls and other lupine features. This new group, in fact, resembles today's red wolf. These wolfish coyotes underwent many changes in the Pleistocene, the most turbulent and intriguing evolutionary epoch.

In the Pleistocene, the only constant factor was change. Ice caps formed, melted, and formed again. Seas rose and fell. Islands appeared and disappeared. From time to time, glaciers would surge over the land like runaway bulldozers, scraping off old hills and throwing up new ones. The Bering land bridge appeared off Alaska, connecting North America to Eurasia, and then it disappeared, leaving the two continents separated again.

Changing climate regimes resulted in changing vegetation, which in turn fostered changes in fauna. Glaciation and other events isolated animal populations long enough to allow them to evolve uniquely.

When circumstances changed, animals that evolved in one region were free to move to other regions. The Pleistocene, in short, was a great goofy laboratory in which evolution could run riot, experimenting with endless possibilities, producing all sorts of beasts.

And what beasts! The experimental animals kicked out of the great Pleistocene experimental laboratory included giant condors, saber-toothed tigers, pigs big enough to sport teeth three feet (1 m) long, and the aurochs, a belligerent bison that managed to survive into the 17th century before disappearing. The Pleistocene also saw multiple tests of the notion that "bigger is better." This was a time of monster elk with freakishly long antlers that reached ten feet (3 m) off the ground. The Pleistocene produced beavers as big as today's brown bears and bears the size of today's grizzlies. Towering over them all was the mammoth, a shaggy elephant that was as big as many of the dinosaurs of the Jurassic period.

Wolves underwent many changes in this seething, complex time. The original wolves – smallish mammals that hardly differed from coyotes – loped across the Bering land bridge to invade Eurasia. They eventually found their way to places as remote as Spain, Japan, and several Middle Eastern countries. Some of those regions still have populations of small, coyotelike wolves.

Meanwhile, a cooling climate in northern Eurasia favored the development of a larger and more formidable wolf. This larger wolf eventually got the chance to return to the North American continent. There it met at least two other wolves, the original coyotelike red wolf and a really fierce animal called the "dire wolf." Dire wolves had massive skulls and formidable teeth. Most dire wolves were significantly larger than today's gray wolves. Dire wolves apparently evolved their unique qualities in South America and later migrated to North America.

These three types of wolf coexisted for some time. The skulls of dire wolves and gray wolves have been found together in California's La Brea tar pits. The dire wolf eventually disappeared, either because it didn't fare well in a time when prey animals were not so large, or possibly because it was eliminated by early humans, who might have seen the dire wolf as a dangerous competitor for their favored prey.

Wolves underwent their most recent evolution in central Alaska in a period when that region was a lush, green refuge surrounded by glaciers. Conditions favored the development of a larger gray wolf. This new type of wolf was eventually freed to spread around the northern hemisphere, invading western Canada, the Rocky Mountains, and much of Siberia.

These large gray wolves that emerged from central Alaska are the most recently developed or "modern" type of wolf. Most wolf populations located far from Alaska represent the earlier (sometimes called "primitive") form of wolf, a type that is smaller, more delicate, and more like coyotes than the gray wolf of Alaska.

Arguments go on. The status of the red wolf has long been controversial, with some authorities thinking it was nothing but a wolf-coyote hybrid. Recently, more taxonomists are crediting the red wolf with being a true species.

The animal currently being debated is the Eastern Canadian gray wolf, or timber wolf (*Canis lupus lycaon*), the wolf often identified with Algonquin Park. Recent research indicates great similarities between this wolf and the red wolf. One researcher has suggested that Canada's Algonquin Park wolf *is* the same animal as the red wolf; others wonder if it might be a hybrid of the red and gray wolf.

Wolves and dogs

While some scientist believe all dogs descended from wolves, others see the relationship as being much more complex. According to them, several different wolf-dog animals appeared at different times and different places in prehistory. Various scientists have offered different speculations about where wolves were domesticated to produce dogs.

The gray wolf evolved into modern form in Alaska. This is the dominant type of wolf in North America now.

Using the power of DNA analysis, scientists have concluded that all dogs descended from a single wolf source. So it apparently was not a common thing for early humans to domesticate wolves. It happened once, and then the products of that early experiment – early dogs – were rapidly distributed because they proved so useful.

And where did that first domestication take place? Dogs from China show greater genetic variation than dogs in other regions, which suggests dogs have existed in Asia longer than anywhere else. This analysis suggests all dogs developed from a single domestication of Chinese wolves approximately 15,000 years ago.

Although all dogs derive from wolves, selective breeding has resulted in an array of dog breeds that resemble wolves to different degrees. Some breeds (sled dogs, huskies, shepherds) are much closer to wolves than others (hounds, terriers, pugs). Many modern dog breeds exhibit such wolfish behavior as caching food, howling at ambulance sirens, and urinating on trees to mark their territories.

Other recent studies have shown that the dogs of the New World derive from that original Eurasian domestication, even though the New World had its own supply of wolves that could have been tamed to produce dogs.

In spite of all the differences that hint at a complicated genetic evolutionary history, dogs and wolves have much in common. The gestation period for red wolves, gray wolves, and dogs is sixty-three days. The most sophisticated genetic sampling techniques can still not differentiate between the DNA of a wolf and a dog.

Genetic similarity does not equate with social compatibility, however. Wolves, dogs, and coyotes frequently kill each other when they meet. That probably results from a basic, timber wolf, but now that wolf is thought to be *Canis lupus nubilis*, a typical gray wolf sometimes called the Great Plains wolf. The large wolf common to Alaska and the Rocky Mountains is *Canis lupus occidentalis*, sometimes called the Rocky Mountain wolf, but increasingly known as the Northern wolf.

The red wolf, *Canis lupus rufus*, is a special case. And as the chapter on red wolves makes clear, its exact status has been highly controversial. Most experts accept the red wolf as a distinct type of wolf, not a subspecies of gray wolf, although some think of it as a gray wolf-coyote hybrid.

Also controversial is the eastern timber wolf, *Canis lupus lycaon*. This is the wolf that lives in southeastern Canada and might have lived in the northeastern region of the US. Once thought to be a gray wolf subspecies, this delicate little wolf is thought by some scientists to be essentially identical to the red wolf. Others think it could be a blend of red and gray wolf.

Arguments about the original range and true nature of subspecies will carry on for a long time, for there isn't much reliable information about early wolves and where they lived. Many wolves, including some possible subspecies, were extirpated before scientists began doing careful work on wolves. Scientific study of wolves started in the 1940s and didn't produce much scholarship until the 1960s.

The red wolf is believed to have originally occurred in many regions of the southeastern US, from coastal Georgia and Florida as far west as Texas. It might have lived as far north as the Carolinas and southern Illinois. But if the Algonquin wolf and red wolf are essentially the same animal, the range of this wolf extended much further north than scientists have believed.

The gray wolf is much more widespread. It originally lived everywhere on the North American continent except for a patch of the southeast that more or less corresponds to the range of the red wolf. Gray wolves, with a few exceptions, occurred almost everywhere in a range that extended as far south as Mexico City and as far north as the Arctic.

Six arenas of controversy

In many ways, the most important distinction between different wolves is not anatomical but political. Speaking politically, North America has six wolf controversies.

The first gray wolf restoration plan was developed for the wolf of the western Great Lakes region, an area that the US Fish and Wildlife Service (USFWS) now refers to as the Eastern Distinct Population Segment (Eastern DPS). This region includes almost a fourth of the US, but in terms of wolf populations, it means Minnesota, Wisconsin, and the Upper Peninsula of Michigan.

A separate recovery plan was put into action in the western US, the region referred to as the Western Distinct Population Segment (Western DPS) by the USFWS, centered in Yellowstone Park. Wolves trapped in Canada were liberated in Yellowstone and central Idaho. The program has been a spectacular success, with wolves flourishing and dispersing into unoccupied territory throughout the West. Of course, wolf opponents fought this plan ferociously, and everything about wolf restoration in the West continues to be controversial.

The USFWS has proposed taking wolves in both the Eastern DPS and Western DPS off the list of endangered species, a process called delisting. That step is highly controversial and is sure to be subjected to several lawsuits.

A third recovery plan has been put into action to restore the highly endangered Mexican wolf (often called the lobo) to a limited bit of land in the Blue Range Wolf Recovery Area in western New Mexico and eastern Arizona. Because of the lobo's genetic uniqueness and rarity, the International Union for Conservation of Nature has placed the highest priority on restoration of Mexican wolves. The program to bring back the lobo has been even more troubled than other wolf restoration plans.

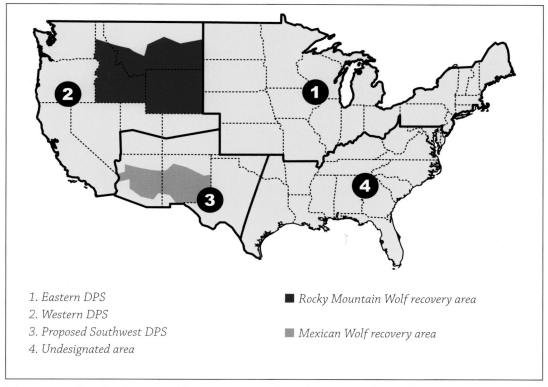

1. Eastern DPS
2. Western DPS
3. Proposed Southwest DPS
4. Undesignated area

■ Rocky Mountain Wolf recovery area

■ Mexican Wolf recovery area

The recovery plans for the gray wolf are now organized into Distinct Populations Segments. Recovery is essentially complete in the Western and Eastern DPS, but has yet to begin in the Southwest DPS.

The red wolf, like the lobo, had to be restored using captive-bred animals. As with the program to restore the Mexican wolf, the restoration plan for red wolves has never envisioned bringing wolves back to a large percentage of its original range. Red wolves now hunt and howl in limited areas of the southeastern US.

Alaska, not surprisingly, represents a unique case. No recovery plan exists for Alaska's wolves because they have never been extirpated or even diminished to a "threatened" status. Alaska's wolves, in fact, continue to flourish. Yet Alaska's wolf management has been the subject of a series of contentious disputes.

Wolf management in Canada has been less controversial, mostly because wolf management hasn't been a major issue in most provinces. That seems to be changing. Canada has no national legislative safeguard like the US's Endangered Species Act, and wolves have survived mostly because there remain significant areas of undeveloped lands where wolves can live in some safety.

Six regions, six wolf controversies. And each is unique and fascinating in its own right.

CHAPTER 4

Meet the Gray Wolf

Gray wolves occur in several colors, and the pelage of most wolves contains a variety of shades and colors. Gray wolves are sometimes not gray, but creamy white or black. A single litter will produce pups whose colors vary. That said, most gray wolves are largely gray on their backs, with warm tan shading on the sides, often with cream legs. The long black guard hairs on the back and shoulders give the gray wolf a grizzled, gray look. The gray wolf face is shaded in contrasting colors that dramatize its changing expressions.

Wolves, in effect, wear two coats. The downy, highly insulating undercoat is thick. When we observe a wolf, however, what we mostly see are the long, glossy guard hairs of the overcoat. Wolf fur has the unusual quality of not accumulating ice when it is struck with warm, moist breath. For this reason, Inuit hunters favor anoraks with wolf fur lining the hood.

The wolf's majestic head frames a pair of eyes that photograph as amber but can seem to change. Lois Crisler, a writer who lived with wolves, described wolf eyes as "level and large and as clear as pure water, gray or gold or green according to mood and individual wolf." People lucky enough to encounter a wolf in the wild are usually struck by the sense of calm power and intelligence in the eyes of the animal.

Among dog breeds, the malamute most closely resembles the wolf. Comparing a wolf to a malamute is a useful way to highlight the differences between wolves and dogs generally. For starters, the wolf's brain is 30 percent larger. The wolf's head, accordingly, is equivalently larger. The wolf's head is distinctly wider, an effect that is accentuated by the long hairs of the "ruff" that flank the wolf's face. The wolf's snout is longer and thinner, possibly because humans have selectively bred dogs to look less threatening than wolves. The wolf's chest is narrow and deeper, and its legs longer. Those long legs terminate in feet that are much larger than those on a dog of the same size (a wolf's foot is comparable in size to a man's balled-up fist). Wolves hold their tails many different ways, but never in the manner of malamutes, curved up over the back.

Wolves are adapted for life in cold climates. When a wolf wraps itself in a ball and tucks its nose in the insulating muff of its tail, it sleeps in apparent comfort in bitterest temperatures. The wolf's body seems designed for a life in deep snow. The narrow chest moves easily in drifts and helps the wolf lay down tracks in a single thin line, which also aids movement in snow. Those great, blocky feet often allow a wolf to run on top of snowdrifts that bog down prey trying to escape on hoofed feet that punch through crusted snow.

A wolf has a formidable set of teeth. Most impressive are the four canines. In an adult wolf, these are over an inch (2.5 cm) in length. Their primary purpose is to puncture the tough hides of such shaggy brutes as moose, giving the wolf a secure grip on a violently thrashing prey animal. The molars at the back of a wolf's mouth can shatter the massive femurs of prey animals as big as bison. Between the canines and the molars are the carnassials, teeth adapted to shear through skin, sinew, and muscle.

Gray wolves are smaller than many people believe. Males weigh between 70 and 110 pounds (32 to 50 kg), with females weighing 60 to 80 pounds (27 to 36 kg). Size relates to geography. The wolves of desert regions may not exceed 45 pounds (20 kg), and the Mexican wolf is small enough to be mistaken for a coyote.

According to a principle known as Bergmann's Law, animals living in cold climates are larger than their counterparts in hot climates. The wolves of Russia and Alaska and the Yukon are the largest. Wolves weighing 115 pounds (52 kg) are not uncommon in these regions, and the rare individual might tip the scales at 175 pounds (77 kg). Because of the bountiful food supply in Yellowstone Park, biologists are seeing something unanticipated and never before documented: *fat* wolves!

In length, wolves approximate the height of humans, ranging from five to six-and-a-half feet (150 to 195 cm), nose to tail tip. Of that length, about 18 inches (46 cm) is tail. Male wolves stand 26 to 32 inches (66 to 81 cm) at the shoulder, so an average human could straddle a wolf at its shoulders.

The wolf's senses

Scientists don't know a great deal about the sensory capabilities of wolves. Serious wolf study only began a few decades ago, and most research has focused on issues of population dynamics. The senses of an animal are tricky to research, and often the potency of a sense must be inferred from indirect evidence.

While a blind wolf wouldn't survive long, scientists consider vision the least developed of a wolf's senses. Vision becomes important to wolves primarily when prey is near. Wolves can

Explosive speed and big feet enable wolves to kill their prey even in deep snow.

detect moving objects at distances where they could not see stationary objects. They see well in conditions of low light, which is important to an animal that often moves at night. Wolves have an uncanny ability to spot signs of vulnerability in prey. Packs often force prey animals to run and then study them for subtle hints of weakness. That obviously involves the sense of sight, but also must depend on a remarkable ability to process and interpret the data their eyes are gathering.

A wolf's sense of hearing is at least as acute as that of humans and probably much keener. A wolf's scoop-shaped external ear funnels vibrations toward the inner ear much like a person who cups a hand behind an ear. Wolves detect howls six miles (10 km) away, possibly as far as ten miles (16 km) away in open terrain. They discriminate between tones that are very similar.

Biologists claim that wolves have a sense of smell that is 100 times more acute than a human's. That is a crude way of indicating that the sense of smell is exquisitely developed in

Wolves have long canine teeth that help them secure a grip on their prey.

wolves. Scent almost surely plays a larger role in the life of a wolf than we understand. Because human observers are oblivious to scents that seem powerful to wolves, even trained observers cannot appreciate all the ways scent affects a wolf's behavior. The significance of scent to wolves can be inferred from the fact they define their territories by using scent markers. Wolves probably rely upon smell as much as humans rely upon sight as a primary way of perceiving their world.

Wolves are one of the most intelligent creatures in the animal kingdom, although we are obliged to deduce this from anecdotes. A retired wolf trapper described how wolves would occasionally hit a snare but escape it by dodging backward quickly. When that happened, he said, he could pick up all his snares from the area because he wouldn't catch any wolves

from that pack. After one wolf learned about snares, the entire pack would become wary.

Captive wolves have learned to escape from their enclosures, sometimes becoming almost impossible to keep confined. These Houdinis do not escape through random effort but by using remarkable problem-solving powers. I recently observed a wolf trying to escape a holding pen. The wolf hurled itself in the air repeatedly, snapping its jaws in an effort to snag a white rope dangling overhead. That rope opened the door to the enclosure, something that this wolf had obviously observed and figured out.

Wildlife biologist Cathy Curby was privileged to observe a remarkable example of wolf intelligence. Curby had been observing a pack of Alaskan wolves through a spotting scope. The mother wolf lay down some distance from the den, where her pups were waiting her return. She seemed reluctant to go to the den. Another wolf, one Curby dubbed "the babysitter," stood by. The two wolves looked at each other without making vocalizations, but apparently the babysitter understood it should go fetch the pups.

It approached the den, played with the pups, then led the way across some rough terrain to where the mother lay waiting. But the pups didn't follow. The babysitter returned to the pups, played with them, then led the way again to their mother. Once more, they didn't follow. The babysitter returned to the pups, then walked away with exaggerated slowness, picking its way with stylized deliberation. The pups followed halfway, then returned to the den. The babysitter went back and tried to push the pups toward their mother. They wouldn't be pushed. The babysitter tried carrying a pup, but the pup got banged on a rock, causing it to squeal and break free. The babysitter sat reflectively for a few moments, then began to trot and hop, yipping playfully, making the "invitation to play" gesture. The excited pups got swept up in the fun of this playful moment, and they didn't notice when the babysitter led them gradually away from the den all the way to the mother.

One pup was left behind, however, and this one obviously felt intimidated about walking through the rough rocks. The babysitter returned to the lost pup. After more reflection, the babysitter set up a game of tug o' war with a bone. The adult wolf and pup played round and round with that bone, moving in crazy circles that gradually led to the mother. Finally the whole family was reunited and suckling contentedly. Curby was so thrilled, she was hopping by her spotting scope, and she has often described the scene in her presentations on wolves.

That babysitter wolf was smart enough to figure out what the mother wanted it to do. Then it was clever enough to come up with five different answers to the problem of how to move the pups. And with that last pup, the babysitter invented yet another technique and found a tool to use to make it work.

Wolves seem especially adept at learning by observation. Some captive wolves learn to open doors with their mouths after observing humans twisting doorknobs. A research assistant once created a machine that dispensed treats when its treadle was manipulated. He trained one wolf on the machine. The next day he was shocked to find that the wolf in the adjacent pen already knew how to use the treadle to dispense treats. The second wolf had been observing the training session through the wire fence.

Because wolves are so intelligent and because they live in packs, the experiences of one wolf can benefit all the others. The ability to learn from observation as well as from each other must have benefited wolves in countless ways over the centuries.

Wolf capabilities

The mobility of wolves is legendary. A Russian proverb claims, "The wolf is fed by his feet." On the tundra, where prey animals are separated by great distances, wolves may travel 40 miles (65 km) a day to feed. A wolf trots at about five miles (8 km) an hour, an easy pace it can maintain for many hours at a stretch. Pressed by hunters, a pack in Finland moved 124 miles (200 km) in one day. Packs have traveled 45 miles (72 km) in a day when not pursued. A wolf is generally on the move eight hours a day, spending about a third of its day trotting or running. Wolves are supremely conditioned athletes.

When launching an attack, a wolf can hit a burst of 35 miles per hour (56 kph). They explode toward their prey in bounds that cover as much as 16 feet (5 m), and it is astonishing to see how quickly a wolf can hit top speed. Wolves can sustain a chase speed of 25 miles per hour (40 kph) for nearly half an hour, although most chases end with a kill or are abandoned in much less time.

Wolves exert a bite pressure of 1,500 pounds per square inch (105 kg/cm^2). That is twice the crunch power of a German shepherd. Wolves can crush bison thighbones more than an inch (3 cm) thick. An average human might find that difficult to do with a sledgehammer on a full swing.

The most aggressive wolves in a pack, the ones that initiate attacks on large prey animals, are particularly liable to be injured. Half the wolves autopsied in an Alaskan study had suffered a previous major injury, such as a broken rib, leg, or fractured skull. The skeleton of one alpha male showed several healed injuries from previous prey encounters, including several broken ribs, a kicked-out tooth, and a fractured jaw. That wolf died when a deer punched its hoof through the wolf's skull.

Wolves are extremely hardy, though, surviving injuries that would kill softer animals. A broken rib or leg means something different for a wolf than for a dog. No veterinarian is going to come along to mend a busted-up wolf, and any wolf stays alive only so long as it continues to be a capable athlete. The sort of nagging injury that might slow up a professional athlete would likely mean death for a wolf.

A Minnesota wolf lived for several years on three legs. When researchers caught her, one back leg was broken and swinging uselessly. After a veterinarian removed the leg, the wolf was released to see if she could carry on in spite of her limitation. That wolf not only survived on three legs but went on to make history as one of the principals in an unusual romantic triangle. The three-legged wolf slipped away from her own pack and had a two-hour "date" with the alpha male from an adjacent pack. To complicate things, her own alpha male apparently mated with another female in his own pack. Such sexual hijinks, common for humans, are rare among wolves.

Decades of federal protection might be teaching wolves living in close proximity to people that they have less to fear from humans.

I photographed that wolf once. She acquired notoriety a second time when she ate some sled dogs owned by famous explorer Will Steger, and then she made history again by becoming the longest-lived wolf in recorded history. She ended her days at a research and educational facility called the Wildlife Science Center near Forest Lake, Minnesota. She was at least 20 years old when she finally died.

Wolves lead strenuous lives while carrying heavy loads of internal and external parasites. Researchers never touch wolf scat with a bare hand because of all the parasite eggs likely to be present. Wolves are capable of fending off a wide range of canine disease that would kill unvaccinated dogs. They have survived gunshots and major injuries that by any reasonable calculation should have been fatal.

So wolves in the wild are lucky to live five or six years, as life is full of risks for them. Any wild wolf ten or older is quite old by wolf standards. In captivity, as we have seen, a wolf 20 years old is exceptionally old.

All the individual senses and abilities of wolves are remarkable enough, yet we underestimate wolves when we consider them piece-by-piece. The wolf is greater than the sum of its parts. Science has yet to find a way to measure the wolf's tenacious grip on life, its ferocious will to live, or its cleverness at learning how to kill without being killed.

Are wolves a threat to humans?

Years ago wolf experts emphatically dismissed old myths about wolves killing humans. They had a mantra: "There is no documented case of a wolf in North America killing a human." Over time, that message had to be modified over and over to account for exceptions, as for example when some captive wolves killed a keeper who entered their enclosure. The mantra kept accumulating qualifiers until it became: "There is no *confirmed* record of an *unprovoked, non-rabid, non-hybrid, wild* wolf in *North America* ever *seriously injuring* a person."

Wolf advocates sometimes overstate the

case that wolves are harmless. They, of course, are partly reacting against the hysteria coming from wolf haters. Fans of wolves are apt to claim that wolves "never have and never will" attack people. A researcher friend recently responded to that by noting that wolves *"probably did, haven't lately, but might again."*

Wolves deserve the respect humans should adopt with all large predators. Such animals as cougars, bears, alligators, and grizzly bears don't routinely attack people, but they are potentially a threat. Wolves are less likely to harm a human than those animals, and yet there is nothing about wolves that guarantees they are harmless. Even "man's best friend," the dog, kills a dozen humans each year.

Researchers have confirmed that gray wolves have preyed upon humans in India, Finland, and France. Wolves have killed or seriously injured 73 children in India alone. A kayaker sleeping on an island off British Columbia was recently attacked by a wolf, incurring a serious bite on his head.

Wolf attack stories should be examined with care. In 1996, in Ontario's Algonquin Park, a wolf grabbed a boy by the head and attempted to pull him from his sleeping bag. The wound required 80 stitches. Yet it isn't clear what the wolf intended. This was a semi-tame animal that often played with campers, running off with tennis shoes and other gear. That wolf might have been trying to be playful.

Another Algonquin wolf, a "super-tame" male that had been photographed almost daily in the summer 1998, made two attacks on children that must be considered close calls. In one case, an alert father stood between the wolf and his little daughter. The wolf kept feinting and trying to get at the child. Two days later the same wolf threw an 11-month old infant three feet into the air. The wolf was driven away and killed by rangers. This was a bold animal that was accustomed to getting food from campers.

In view of several such incidents with super-tame wolves, Algonquin Park officials have altered management protocols. They once tolerated tame wolves because they seemed to offer great chances to dispel myths about wolves. Now tame wolves are removed as a precaution because, as one official put it, "I'd rather remove a wolf before than after it attacks a child."

Why haven't wolves attacked people in the past? They've certainly had no end of opportunities and abundant provocation (think of all the snoopy biologists who have shinnied down dens to count pups). Now that wolves are dispersing into settled regions near their territories, wolves and people are having more frequent encounters. And yet people continue to move safely in "wolf country."

Two facts help explain why wolves so rarely attack people.

First, wolves have learned from bitter experience that humans are deadly. For centuries, humans have killed wolves any time they had a chance to do so. Most wolves flee or cautiously study any human they spot. But this is a wariness supported by what might be called "cultural wisdom" in wolves, knowledge passed on from wolf to wolf. Fear of humans is a learned response, not a genetic trait.

Second, people do not present the visual cues that trigger wolves to attack. An upright human looks, smells, and moves nothing like a deer. In fact, an upright human looks a lot like an angry bear, and wolves don't like to mess with bears. Even if wolves don't perceive upright humans as bears, they might read that upright posture as a sign of dominance. Wolf attacks are often triggered by the flight of a prey animal, especially an animal that does not move with the fluid grace of a healthy individual. Animals that stand tall and hold their ground are rarely attacked. The visual cues given off by most humans are very different from those of, for example, panicky sheep, and that has probably been a good thing for us.

Yet some observers who know wolves believe they might attack and kill a human in North America, given the right circumstances.

Some wolf experts are beginning to believe that decades of governmental protection

Though they are beautiful, wolves are wild animals that should be treated with caution and respect.

might be producing wolves that are not afraid of people. We might be in a new chapter of wolf-human interaction, what might be called the "post-persecution" era. Wolves, after all, are highly intelligent and quick to perceive threat. It would be odd if they did *not* respond to the observable fact that most people are not trying to kill them.

Wolf experts don't expect wolves to suddenly begin attacking humans, yet they sometimes talk about two factors that concern them. If a wolf does attack a human in the next several years, it will almost surely be an animal that has been emboldened by getting food from humans. And if a wolf does make a fatal attack on a human, the victim might likely be a youngster. Wildlife authorities advise parents against allowing toddlers to play unattended in wolf country. It is just common sense.

People used to seeing animals portrayed sympathetically on television are beginning to lose any sense that an animal might be dangerous. Vacationers and cabin owners have recently begun putting food out for bears, seeing them as clownish and harmless. That frequently results in some incident that causes the death of the bear. Sadly, some cabin owners are now trying to do the same with wolves. People who love wolves should never confuse them with pets. Bold, habituated wolves are a threat to people, and habituated wolves are at great risk of being killed when they do something people deem inappropriate.

It is still essentailly true that wolves do not attack people. People hunt, fish, sleep, and camp in wolf country with no reason to be fearful. And it is just as true that wolves are powerful predators that should be treated with the same respect we owe any large, wild predator.

CHAPTER 5

Wolf Society

Wolf experts grimace when they hear people say, "Wolves always . . ." or "Wolves never . . . ." While wolves are orderly creatures that behave according to certain well-understood principles, they're also flexible and difficult to predict. Wolves are highly social animals. Much of a wolf's personality is learned, not genetically programmed as a fixed instinct. This makes wolves less stereotyped in their behavior than most animals. It also makes them fascinating.

Much of what we thought we knew about wolf behavior has come in for a shakeup recently. The wolves of the Lamar Valley of Yellowstone Park are more easily observed than any wolf pack in history, and they seem to be behaving naturally. And yet these highly visible wolves have delighted and confounded wolf experts by doing unexpected things.

The wolf personality

It is difficult to generalize about the "wolf personality." We don't always know which personality traits are inherited and which have been acquired through learning. For example, wolves have often been described as fearful around humans as if that were a fixed trait. But that shyness might be the natural response to centuries of persecution. Any trait acquired through learning might be unlearned if circumstances change. Observers believe wolves are becoming bolder in the areas around the western Great Lakes, just as the wolves of Denali and Yellowstone Park are becoming comfortable around humans.

Second, social animals like wolves don't all have the same personality. This only makes sense. After all, dogs – even dogs from the same litter – exhibit highly diverse personalities. While wolves by nature always try to ascend in the pack hierarchy, some individuals are quick to accept lower status while others seem fiercely driven to rise to the top. To some extent, the personality of the alphas will affect the personalities of all the wolves in that pack. A highly aggressive pair of alphas, for example, can cause the whole pack to act belligerently. Mellow alphas lead mellow wolf packs.

Third, a wolf's personality changes as the animal matures and assumes different roles in the pack. Pack leaders are generally decisive, outgoing, and self-confident. Underlings are obsequious and loyal to the alphas. Some low-ranking adults have distinctively goofy, playful personalities, blending aspects of the puppy personality with adult traits. A low-ranking member that graduates and assumes an alpha role will exhibit a remarkable change, acquiring some version of the classic, self-assured alpha character.

With all those qualification, what can we say about the wolf personality? The key to understanding wolves is to understand the social dynamics of the pack.

For the pack to adhere and function, its members must live cooperatively. Adolph Murie wrote, "The strongest impression remaining with me after watching the wolves on numerous occasions was their friendliness." Reunions between pack members are celebrated with a display of joy that has been called "the jubilation of wolves."

Pack members cooperate extensively. Wolves work as a team when hunting. Low-ranking members sometimes perform "babysitting" chores, and all pack members might feed the pups. At times, pack members have nurtured injured wolves. In Alaska, a wolf caught in a trap was apparently fed for days by other pack members. However, in the same circumstances, trapped wolves have sometimes been killed and eaten by their own pack.

Conflict within the pack is abnormal and deeply disturbing to wolves. That's hardly surprising, since social discord is incompatible with the efficient functioning of the pack. One of Lois Crisler's wolves was so distressed when it witnessed a fight that it separated the combatants, yanking one back by the tail. A good deal of snapping and snarling is common within packs, but serious aggression is not. Having each pack member slotted in terms of status is a way of avoiding discord.

Close observation of wolves has totally changed the way we think of them.

Researcher Dave Mech has speculated that the range of different personalities in a pack might give it stability. If all wolves were essentially the same but differed only in innate cockiness, to take one example, pack members might have to waste time and energy sorting out the hierarchy. Having multiple personality types in each pack might lead to less aggression and more stability.

Wolves are so docile in some situations that people have ignorantly called them "cowardly." Many wolves caught in a leg-hold trap, for example, are oddly compliant. What accounts for this lack of fight in an animal with the stunning power and destructive potential of a wolf? One reason is that wolves live in hierarchies. They are programmed to dominate underlings but to respect alphas. A self-confident human must look like an alpha animal to wolves. This tendency of wolves to "read" human body language is just one of the ways the human-wolf relationship is fascinating.

People and wolves

The readiness of wolves to view humans as fellow wolves shows up frequently in wolf literature. Lois Crisler and her husband found that they could communicate with their pet wolves by adopting wolf body language. Lori Schmidt, who has for many years maintained captive wolves for the International Wolf Center in Ely, Minnesota, used to make a game of anticipating which humans her wolves would dislike. The alpha males would sometimes single out the most self-confident male and attempt to keep him at a distance. Other times, the wolves objected to "flaky" people and persons with particularly low self-esteem. Writer R. D. Lawrence once was told by a person who visited schools with an ambassador wolf on a leash that the wolf would sometimes growl quietly at a child. Invariably, the wolf's manager said, the teacher would later identify that child as an outcast who was not accepted well by the other children.

A biologist once told me about one of these ambassador wolves that was so friendly it was a big favorite in school classrooms. Then one day the handler noted that the wolf's attitude toward children changed. It was pacing and looking at the children in a way that suggested it was measuring them for a meal. That wolf was quickly retired from ambassadorial duties. What caused that change? The wolf's handler traced the new response to the moment a child threw a temper tantrum, flailing at the floor with his arms and legs. At about the same time, that wolf met an autistic child. Something about those two children conveyed a message to this wolf something like, "I am out of control. I am unfit." Those are the same signals wolves get from panicky sheep, signals that can trigger attacks. This wolf never misbehaved, but its sensitive handler might have been right that it had learned to see children as potential prey.

Relations and communications between wolves and humans can take strange turns. A friend, Peggy Callahan, learned from a wolf that she was pregnant. Callahan directs the Wildlife Science Center, near Forest Lake, Minnesota. The center maintains a variety of wildlife, including many wolves, for research projects and for educating the public about wildlife. One day she encountered strange behavior from a wolf she had raised from a puppy. After greeting her, this wolf began to offer food to her, although he had never done this before during a close relationship that spanned seven years. So insistent was the wolf that she finally felt compelled to pretend to eat a deer leg the wolf brought her. Only then did he leave her alone. When Peggy later confirmed that she was pregnant, she decided that the wolf had sensed it before she did.

Wolves are not sloppy in their social relations. They live in a highly structured social system and take pains to respect the integrity of that system. Each wolf knows precisely where it ranks and what actions it may or may not take.

Wolves are usually hostile toward wolves

dispersing from other packs. A pack will often kill a wolf that wanders into its territory, and sometimes adjacent packs go to war with each other. At other times, wolves can switch from one pack to another and be accepted by the new pack. This unpredictability about the ways wolves respond to outsiders might be related to food abundance, or it might simply reflect the variability of the personalities of the wolves involved. Researchers have recently learned that some of these cases of adjacent packs living harmoniously involve wolves that are biologically related to at least one wolf in the other pack. If a wolf from an adjacent pack is a daughter or sister of the alpha of another pack, it might be permitted to "visit" without sparking aggression.

People who admire wolves and idealize them are sometimes discomfited by all the aggression wolves display toward each other. Yet this is simply the way wolves organize their social lives. The normal way a wolf in the wild dies is by starvation or being killed by other wolves. Alien packs and even unattached single wolves represent a threat to a resident pack, so they are often dealt with harshly. In this regard, as in many others, wolf packs resemble human street gangs, offering their own members affection and support, while exhibiting territorialism, violence, and intolerance toward outsiders.

The hostility of wolves toward outsiders may explain why they kill coyotes and dogs. Wolves that are raised with dogs will view the dogs as fellow pack members. But wild wolves that encounter a coyote or dog will usually attack and kill it. One unfortunate consequence of wolf restoration is the beloved pets lost to wolves.

The pack

A wolf pack is essentially an extended family. Most packs consist of a dominant breeding pair and any number of their offspring. Of course, it isn't that simple – very little about wolves is! Some packs include "aunts" and "uncles." Occasionally a unrelated wolf attaches to a pack. Now and then an alpha wolf lives long enough to be toppled from its throne by a more vigorous young pack member. The old wolf might remain a pack member, albeit one with reduced status.

A wolf pack is not a loose assemblage of animals, but a tightly knit unit. Pack members might hunt alone, but commonly hunt together and spend a great deal of their time with each other.

Biologists have names for different classes of pack members. The cocky, happy leaders who do all the breeding are the "alphas." Adult wolves below the alphas are known as "betas" or "biders," (referring to the fact they are biding their time, waiting for a chance to rise in status). In large packs, there might also be some unfortunate animal that serves as the scapegoat or "omega" wolf. Omegas are abused by most of the pack. Wolf pups enjoy a privileged position that is not, strictly speaking, above or below other pack members. The whole pack is likely to shower the pups with affection and attention, at least until they grow up. Sometimes a pack member assumes the role of special caretaker for the pups.

There are two lines of dominance, one male and one female. The alpha male enforces the male dominance line, and the alpha female enforces the female line. Alpha females are often aggressive in defense of their exclusive right to breed. There are documented cases of mothers killing daughters in fights over breeding rights.

Wolves engage in many small acts of aggression that continually reinforce the clarity of the social order. Dominant wolves pick on lower animals at random moments for no apparent reason except to demonstrate that they have the right to do so. Many of these demonstrations come at feeding times. All this seemingly gratuitous conflict looks ugly to humans, but it keeps wolf packs coherent and free of serious conflict.

Researchers no longer claim that wolf packs are always led by males, or even that a pack has a single leader. In many situations, such as

Within a pack, wolves' relationships are tight and highly structured. They always know where they stand.

when choosing a route or deciding to attack a prey animal, one wolf clearly takes the lead. In the past, most observers assumed that the leader was the alpha male. But the alpha female is just as apt to lead. And at times, leadership is shared by the whole pack. Dave Mech once observed a leader abandon a plan that proved to be unpopular with the rest of the pack.

Packs can number as few as two wolves or as many as thirty. Most packs have between five and ten wolves. In Alaska and northern Canada, packs run larger.

And packs are always changing size. A pack achieves maximum size when a fresh cohort of pups is added, then dwindles as wolves leave or die. Mortality is especially high among pups. Because pups die at such high rates, wolf managers maintain separate counts on adults and pups. Population estimates are based on adults alone.

Pack size seems correlated with prey size, but the relationship is complex. Wolves that prey on small animals typically live in small groups. Those who prey primarily on deer usually form packs of four to six wolves. Wolves preying on moose often run in packs of fourteen to sixteen members. People have usually assumed the larger packs helped the wolves take down large, dangerous prey, and yet there actually is no advantage to wolves in having such a large pack to kill large prey. The killing is usually done by two or three particularly skillful hunters, with the rest of the pack doing little more than cheerleading. Pack size has little to do with killing and more to do with the efficient utilization of the food once it is killed.

Recent research correlates pack size with the

need to protect a kill against scavengers, especially ravens. Researchers on Isle Royale have documented a single wolf killing a moose on eleven occasions, so packs of eighteen wolves are not strictly needed to bring down a large ungulate. Ravens are exceptionally aware of their environment, often showing up at a wolf kill while the prey is still bleeding. Individual ravens can carry off four pounds of meat in a day. A pair of wolves might lose 37 percent of a moose kill to ravens, whereas a pack of six wolves would lose only 17 percent. Hunting in packs could thus be the way wolves make the best use of their kills.

Pack coherence is dynamic, not static. Life in a pack offers each member certain survival advantages, so wolves are strongly motivated to stay within their packs. Yet all pack members below the alphas sacrifice self-interest to live in the pack. They defer to the alphas in such matters as breeding rights and access to food. To some extent, self-interest and group coherence are in conflict; thus there are always centrifugal and centripetal forces acting on a pack. When the pack grows too large, stress sets in, the center no longer holds and the pack might split.

Communication

A social animal cannot afford fuzzy communications. For example, a wolf must be able to discriminate between a bluff and a serious status challenge. While wolves cannot make speeches or send instant messages to each other, they make themselves understood with a combination of vocalizations, body language, and scent.

Wolves growl, squeal, bark, whine, and (of course) howl. Whimpering or whining is a way of conveying friendly intentions. Lois Crisler referred to whimpering when she described her wolves "talking." She wrote, "The wolf talking is deeply impressive, because the wolf is so emotionally stirred. His eyes are brilliant with feeling." Growling is a threatening noise. Barks signal alarm.

Wolf howls are one of the most moving and haunting sounds in nature. An old trapper described a pack howl as "a dozen train whistles braided together." Wolves throw themselves into howling with evident joy. Crisler compared howling to a "community sing." She added, "Wolves love a howl. When it is start-

ed, they instantly seek contact with one another, troop together, fur to fur. Some wolves . . . will run from any distance, panting and bright-eyed, to join in, uttering, as they near, fervent little wows, jaws wide, hardly able to wait to sing."

Each howling wolf sings a unique note. When Crisler howled with her wolves she learned that if she trespassed on the note a wolf was singing, it would shift up or down a

Body language tells us these two pack members are expressing subordinate allegiance to an alpha wolf.

pitch or two. "Wolves avoid unison singing," Crisler noted. "They like chords." Possibly, but biologists believe the function of polyphonic singing is to amplify the impact of the howl. Wolves singing two different notes produce three tones – the two being sung, plus a harmonic. Fred Harrington, a researcher who worked extensively with howling, noted that an observer can distinguish between one and two howling wolves, but "any more than two sound like a dozen."

Ulysses S. Grant and a guide once heard a stirring chorus of wolf howls. The guide asked how many animals were making that sound. Grant wanted to prove he was no dude. Although he was certain that so much sound could only be coming from a large pack, Grant announced that "just 20" wolves were howling. The men rode up on the pack. Two wolves sat on their haunches, their upturned mouths held close together like barbershop quartet singers.

Howling celebrates and reinforces pack unity. In that regard, wolves resemble such human packs as street gangs or athletic teams, which have their own solidarity rituals. It is accurate – if a little fanciful – to translate some group howls as communicating something like: "We're the Mink Lake Pack, and we're alright! Trespassers here are in for a fight!"

Like *aloha*, the howl of a wolf has many different potential meanings defined by context. Wolves howl to reinforce territorial claims, particularly when challenged by an intruding pack. Fred Harrington concluded that wolves howl most readily when they have something to defend, such as pups in a den or a fresh kill. Pack members howl back and forth to keep track of each other when visual communication isn't possible. A howling session can reunite a pack that has broken up to hunt within an area.

Sometimes packs howl as if to celebrate a kill. This might be a way of keeping intruders away from the kill, or it might be the wolf equivalent of "high fives." At times, wolves just seem to howl to express themselves. It sounds like anthropomorphizing to say so, yet careful observers have often witnessed wolves moaning in apparent misery after the death of pups or a mate.

Wolves respond to human howls, something documented for the first time when Tolstoy wrote about it in 1862. Researchers often howl to trigger a reply that will confirm the presence of a pack in a certain area. This willingness of wolves to reply to human howls has led to a new form of tourism. Many groups and agencies now sponsor howling trips to known pack locations. After all, howling to wolves is about the only way for a wolf fan to experience direct contact with a wild wolf. It is deeply thrilling to howl into the darkness and then be overwhelmed by the answer of a wolf. Of course, the wolf might be saying the equivalent of, "Buzz off, dammit!" But the wolf is talking to you, which is heady stuff.

Body language and facial expressions help wolves maintain the clarity of social status. As noted earlier, the faces of wolves are shaded in ways that highlight their changing expressions (for example, their black gums contrast starkly with their white teeth). Like mimes or clowns, wolves have plastic, variable faces that are marked to dramatize changing emotions. Most facial expressions communicate one type of message, which is the degree to which a wolf is feeling aggressive or submissive. In the context of pack interactions, that is *the* critical issue for wolves.

Various body postures also allow wolves to communicate. A wolf saying "hello" drops its head to the ground, exposing its neck in an act of submission. Dominant wolves intimidate lesser pack members with fixed stares. In wolf society, making direct eye contact is an aggressive act, not good manners. Wolves also express dominance by such gestures as standing up to ride across the back of other wolves. People who have owned playful dogs will recognize the bowing, high rump, low head posture known as the "invitation to play."

A wolf's tail is a semaphore that signals the animal's attitude. For example, high tails indicate dominance and high spirits. Submissive animals tuck their tails tightly under their bellies. Even untrained observers can spot dominant and submissive wolves by noting the messages being sent by their tails. Researchers have identified 11 distinct tail postures, each conveying a specific message to other wolves in the area.

Scent is the wolves' third medium for social communication. Scientists know less about scent's importance in communication because, unlike other forms of discourse, scent cannot be perceived directly by human researchers. Researchers must infer its function by watching wolves respond to its presence.

Alpha wolves of both sexes raise their legs to urinate, spraying scent high, where it will be conspicuous. Lesser pack members of both sexes squat like female dogs to urinate. Urine depositions mark the boundaries of a pack's territory. Like spray-painted graffiti of street gangs, these "Keep Out!" signs are particularly dense where the territorial boundaries of adjacent packs come close together.

Scent helps wolves navigate their territories. Wolves leave scent-marks at significant points, such as trail junctions, creating olfactory points of reference.

Trappers used to believe that wolves moved around their territories in rigid patterns, such as always moving counterclockwise. Researchers now know that wolves create and retain superb mental maps that allow them to dive off a familiar trail and beeline cross-country to a particular destination.

Other uses of scent are more obscure. Wolves often defecate near such man-made objects as discarded pop cans. Wolf trappers traditionally hated finding piles of dung beside their meticulously disguised trap sets. They thought the wolves were mocking their professional skills. A more plausible interpretation is that the dung simply marks a new or alien object that a wolf finds in its territory.

Territory

Territorialism is not understood as well as other aspects of wolf biology because it is expensive to study. Many research assistants must monitor many wolves wearing many collars for long periods of time to learn where wolves do and do not travel. Some of this research is now being done with radio collars that can be monitored by satellite, although neither the collars nor the satellites are cheap.

People tend to think wolf territories are semipermanent areas with stable borders, like the borders of nation states. This is misleading. Territories sometimes overlap. More often, adjacent territories are not contiguous, like national borders, but are separated by "buffer zones."

Territorial borders also fluctuate, changing shape as a pack changes size. There may even be a seasonal dimension to territories, so habitat defended by a pack in February might not be worth defending in June. Like so many aspects of wolf society, the issue of territory is subject to constant revision.

It is clear that wolves need a lot of living space. Whereas a deer might live in a territory of less than half a square mile (1.3 km^2), most wolf packs defend territories of 50 to 150 square miles (130 to 388 km^2). The size of wolf territories is a direct reflection of the density of the prey base. The smallest area that can support a pack in good deer country is about 30 square miles (78 km^2), whereas packs in Arctic areas are thinly populated by prey animals, so wolves there need territories as large as 1,000 square miles (2,590 km^2). Some packs in elk-rich Montana are prospering in territories of less than 20 square miles (52 km^2).

Bob Cary, a long-time observer of wolves, describes wolf territories in northeastern Minnesota as resembling Swiss cheese, with the holes representing established territories and the cheese representing buffer zones. Cary has learned he has better chances of bagging a deer for his family if he hunts the cheese and avoids the holes.

CHAPTER 6

A Year in the Life of a Pack

For wolves, the year breaks down into two markedly different halves. During most of fall and winter, the pack lives on the run. In spring and summer, the pack has a more or less fixed address while it concentrates on raising a new generation of wolves.

The annual pattern described here applies to most wolves, but not all. Some wolves, for example ones that depend on caribou, have evolved a different lifestyle, following the great herds as they migrate.

The pantry

The wolf's reproductive cycle is synchronized to take advantage of seasonal food abundance. Wolves depend primarily on ungulates. Deer and moose typically have a hard time in late winter. They enter the spring in poor condition, making them vulnerable to wolves at just the time when wolves need a reliable source of nutrition for their pups.

Denning wolves must do all of their hunting in a limited area, rather than roaming freely as they do the rest of the year. Most ungulates give birth in late spring. Newborn moose, caribou, and deer are vulnerable. Thus the wolves' pantry is restocked with a fresh bounty of young ungulates at the moment when the pack is limited to hunting the territory around its den.

That bounty doesn't last, however. As wolves and other predators make repeated withdrawals from the supply of prey animals, finding food becomes more of a challenge. The pantry has less and less to offer wolves as the year progresses. There is reason to believe that beaver is more important to wolves than once was thought. In areas with good beaver populations, beaver might constitute as much as three-fourths of the wolves' diet in spring and summer, a time when wolves have more than the usual trouble hunting the big ungulates they usually rely upon for food.

The last wild wolf I observed was also the sorriest looking wolf I've seen. This was near the end of summer, not a great time for wolves. This animal looked miserable as it slunk along a county highway, occasionally leaving the blacktop to forage for road-killed animals. The wolf ignored my minivan, just a few feet behind it, as it scavenged. It looked hot and bug-bedeviled, and its body language said that this wolf couldn't wait for cold weather and snow to come again.

Most "lone wolves" are young dispersers. They face high risks when they leave the security of the pack.

Dispersers

Now and then, a young wolf decides to strike off on its own. A bider becomes a disperser. Many dispersers are yearlings, although a young wolf might bide for a year or two before deciding to take off. Both sexes disperse.

These defections from the pack are remarkable. Wolves are social animals, so a lone animal is a wolf living in an atypical way. It must be difficult for a wolf to sever the emotional ties that have held it to the pack. Some dispersers need to work up to the schism by undertaking a series of short experimental separations.

Dispersing also exposes a wolf to great hazards. Acquiring food is difficult and dangerous enough for a pack, so the lone wolf scavenges or hunts at a huge disadvantage. Dispersers risk blundering into the territory of a wolf pack that might protect its borders with deadly force. Dispersers move through territory

they do not know, encountering humans and their vehicles at unexpected moments. For all these reasons, mortality among dispersers is high.

Why would a wolf disperse if it is so risky and difficult? Some young wolves simply get fed up with low status. In particular, they might resent being denied the freedom to breed. Researchers point to the fact that dispersers often leave shortly before the mating season, a time of exceptional tension in the pack. While it can be misleading to compare wolves to humans, one can think of a young wolf as something akin to a 20-year-old human still obliged to live at home. That young human might sulk and think, "Man, I gotta get outta here! Mom and Dad get all the best food. Everyone picks on me. And they don't let me have any sex!"

No single pattern applies to all dispersers. Some remain within their former pack's territory. Others take off on a beeline as if they had a compass, a map, and some distant objective. Dispersers can travel astonishing distances, as much as 120 miles (193 km) in a single day. One wolf traveled over 500 miles (805 km) before finding what it was seeking. Sometimes a disperser drifts into a buffer zone between pack territories. Now and then, a disperser meets a resident pack that accepts it as a new member. Being accepted might happen more often when the dispersing wolf is related to a member of the new pack.

Dispersing wolves are looking for unoccupied territory and a mate. Some lucky dispersers succeed in both objectives, although many more must take their chances and suffer the consequences of failure. These happy meetings of two lucky dispersers is the main way wolves form new packs.

The dispersal mechanism ensures that wolves make the best possible use of their habitat. When conditions are favorable for wolves (mainly when food is abundant), dispersers survive and form new packs. They then start filling new habitat with more young wolves. When conditions are adverse, dispersers die. Their removal from the pack reduces the amount of food required to keep it going, bringing the number of predators more in line with what the habitat can provide. Dispersing also minimizes genetic problems that might arise from inbreeding.

Courtship and reproduction

Each year, a wolf pack must renew its claim on the future by offsetting attrition with reproduction. But since overpopulation is as threatening to wolves as inadequate recruitment, several devices limit the animal's reproductive potential so wolf numbers have a good chance of being in balance with the available prey.

Wolves do not usually reach sexual maturity and reproduce until they are three, four, or five years old. Some wolves reproduce when they are two, and a few well-fed zoo wolves have reproduced when just a year old. Wild wolves generally reach sexual maturity earlier when food is abundant, when the pack has suffered high mortality, or when there is abundant habitat that could absorb more wolves. In other words, rather than being rigidly fixed, wolf sexual maturity is flexible and tied to various factors. Wolves, in this way, have a number of efficient "shock absorbers" that function to keep wolf numbers aligned with the capacity of the habitat to support them.

The main limitation on reproduction is social. The alpha male denies other males access to the breeding female, just as she jealously prevents other females for mating with the alpha male. People, for decades, have spoken approvingly of the fact wolves "mate for life," and there are touching examples of wolves that have sustained affectionate bonds for many years and are disconsolate when a partner dies. However, as researchers gain more detailed information about wolf sexual habits, they are beginning to see that wolves "fool around" outside the sacred alpha pair bond more than we used to know.

Mating and denning

As a result of the social structure that limits breeding rights, most wolf packs produce one litter a year. Some packs include a second breeding female and thus a second litter of pups. Pups from second litters don't enjoy the same prospects for survival as the alpha's litter. Second litters are another way in which wolf numbers are kept in line with the food abundance of the habitat. These second litters, based on observations at Yellowstone, might be more common than researchers formerly thought, and there have even been cases of third litters. The best guess might be that these multiple litters are triggered by the exceptionally abundant prey in Yellowstone.

In the weeks before mating, the breeding pair engages in a number of affectionate gestures. The alphas groom and nuzzle each other. Less romantically, they perform "RLUs" (raised leg urinations). When the female is in estrus, her urine is bloody. Researchers monitoring wolf populations look for double urine marks in the winter snow, one bloody. That is a sign that another litter of wolf pups will soon be suckling in a nearby den.

The mating season can be protracted over a period of weeks in late winter and spring. Northern wolves mate later than southern wolves, probably because northern ungulates produce their offspring later in the year. Breeding couples sometimes slip away to couple in privacy. This isn't modesty; they just want to get away from all the interference from the pesky, nonbreeding wolves.

Very little about wolf biology is cut-and-dried. Sometimes the alpha male or female does not choose to participate in breeding. Nobody knows why. Mated pairs are usually faithful for as long as both are alive, but not always. The more detailed information researchers gain about wolf behavior, the more they discover it is unpredictable. Wolves do well because they are intelligent and have a high reproductive potential, but it is also true that wolf biology and wolf society are marked by exceptional flexibility, and that is surely one of the reasons wolves have done so well in so many places.

After breeding, the female seeks a den. Den sites are often used year after year, and some have been used every spring for many decades. The den Adolph Murie discovered in Alaska in the 1940s is still producing young wolves today. If a female cannot find a suitable den, she digs one. She might evict some smaller animal from its home and enlarge the domicile to suit her needs. Or she might just settle for a depression in the ground.

Dens are usually caves, holes in the ground, or chambers formed by jumbles of rocks. A den must be dry and secure, situated in good hunting territory, and located near water. Wolves seem to prefer den sites near high ground, so they can survey their surroundings and spot potential threats to the precious pups. While lounging in elevated areas might help them

spot approaching danger, researchers also note that wolves just seem to enjoy a good view while they are resting.

Pups

Wolf pups are born 63 days after the breeding pair mates. Litters range in size from three to nine pups, but four to six is the most common. The pug-nosed pups are born blind, deaf, and capable of only a limited amount of scooting around to take advantage of the warmth of their mother. Newborn pups weigh about a pound (450 g) but grow with astonishing speed. Wolf pups can gain three pounds (1.4 kg) a week. Humans who raise wolf pups say they almost seem to increase in size as you watch them.

At the age of several weeks, wolf pups are so winsome that they have been known to melt the hearts of the professional wolf hunters. One such "wolfer" wrote, "I have never had to do anything that goes against the grain more than to kill the pups at this stage. Potential murderers they may be, but at this time they are just plump, friendly little things that nuzzle you and whine little pleased whines."

At about three weeks, pups begin venturing into the outside world. They romp at the den mouth and begin play fighting. At this age, the tiny wolves form bonds with the rest of the pack.

All pack members involve themselves with the care of the pups. Even the alpha male will exhibit unusual tolerance for their tomfoolery. In zoos, some unbred female wolves have undergone hormonal changes known as "pseudo pregnancy," later producing milk and nursing the young. Such wet-nursing has not been confirmed among wild wolves, but it might take place. Low-ranking pack members often become "aunts" and "uncles" and develop special babysitter relationships with the pups.

Wolves introduce pups to solid food in an ingenious way. Each day, pack members radiate out from the den to hunt, while the mother remains at home to care for her offspring. Suc-

Pack members bring food back to the pups by eating and later disgorging it.

cessful hunters fill up with meat, then return to the den, where they disgorge a meal for the pups and nursing mother. The disgorged food provides pups with tenderized, chopped-up meat that their young digestive systems can handle. Later on, pack member bring un-chewed chunks of meat, like the haunch of a deer, to the pups.

Starting very early in life, little wolves engage in endless hours of roughhousing. All the pouncing, stalking, wrestling, and fighting serves two critical functions. The pups are acquiring skills they will need when they begin to hunt prey in earnest. And at the same time, they are establishing their own dominance hierarchy.

When the pups reach about nine weeks of age, they're mobile enough to permit the pack to move to a "rendezvous site." Dave Mech describes these as "essentially a den above ground." Rendezvous sites are secure areas near water, like dens. If the pack makes a kill, the adults may move the pups to the kill site rather than the other way around, which is another way of creating a rendezvous site.

Sometime in early fall, the pack hits the trail again, with the pups running along. Though these youngsters are now full-sized and look like adults, they can do little more than cheer from the sidelines during attacks on dangerous prey. All in all, the first year of life for a young wolf is a harsh sort of school. Young wolves that do not receive passing grades are not around for long.

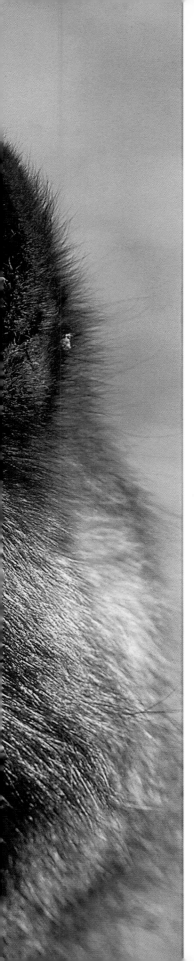

CHAPTER 7

Wolves and Their Prey

It seems so simple: Surround a deer, cut it down, and then *bon appetit!* But for wolves, acquiring food is anything but easy. While animals that feed on vegetation can expect to eat their fill just about every day, wolves often go several days – even weeks – between meals. Their meals run away from them and then put up dangerous fights.

No dainty eater

Wolves do indeed "wolf" their food. Four wolves were once seen consuming most of a mule deer in four hours. A wolf can bolt down a meal of 18 pounds (8 kg) of meat – the equivalent of a man downing a 40-pound (18-kg) steak – at one sitting. Hungry wolves eat until their bellies are stretched, then lie down to digest and sleep. Then they might get up and do it all over again. It is the eating pattern of an animal accustomed to feast-famine cycles. Indian hunters used to tell tales of sneaking up on "meat-drunk" wolves.

The wolf's digestive system is adapted for processing food quickly. Because its metabolism runs at such a hot pace, a wolf must drink copious amounts of water to avoid uremic poisoning. That's one reason that den sites and wolf travelways are usually near water.

Wolves consume as much of their prey as they can as quickly as they can. They usually leave behind only a few scraps of hide, the skull, and possibly part of the stomach contents. After a kill, the pack either camps at the site or revisits the carcass until even the bony lower legs are eaten. By the time a pack abandons a kill, virtually nothing remains to show that an animal weighing as much as 1,000 pounds (454 kg) was consumed on this spot. That is troublesome when wolves attack livestock, for most compensation programs depend on some proof that wolves were responsible for the loss of the animals. Particularly when wolves go after sheep, there might not be much more left than a fluffy bit of wool drifting on the wind.

In the process of devouring their prey, wolves swallow large amounts of bone and hair. Veterinarians tell dog owners they should never feed bones to their pets because sharp bone ends can puncture stomach or intestinal tissue. In a wolf's stomach, however, sharp objects are spun in hair until the dangerous bone is wrapped in a soft cushion.

That explains the mystery of the wolf scat that contained a Mepps

Spinner. The Mepps is a popular fishing lure with exceptionally sharp treble hooks. It apparently passed through a wolf without causing injury because the hooks were encased in a felt-like mass of hair.

That leaves us wondering how a fishing lure got in a wolf in the first place. We can only guess, but here is a likely scenario. The wolf in this odd story had a habit of checking out a heron rookery to see if a dead baby bird or some other food item might have been kicked out of the nests above. Perhaps a fish – like a young northern pike – grabbed that Mepps Spinner and bit through the line with its teeth. A heron could have seen the pike struggling in the water with the spinner caught in its gills or throat. Imagine that heron then serving the hapless fish to its young before pitching the bony head of the fish out of the nest. Along came the wolf, who ate the head, spinner and all.

What wolves eat

Wolves aren't fussy eaters, although they are decidedly carnivorous. They'll consume almost any meat they can acquire, including birds, fish, hares, lizards, mice, insects, and worms. The willingness of wolves to eat rotten carrion suggests that their energy budget is too stringent to allow them to bypass an easy meal.

A common interest in carrion is part of the bond between wolves and ravens. Ravens are so quick to get to a wolf kill, they often arrive while the prey is still warm. One way researchers locate wolves is by looking under raucous flocks of ravens. Ravens must return the favor, if unwillingly, by occasionally leading wolves to carrion.

As mentioned, the main prey for wolves is large ungulates: moose, elk, sheep, deer, caribou, bison, or musk oxen. But beaver can be very important during summer months.

Predator-prey relations

One of the most complicated and controversial aspects of wolf biology is the impact wolves have on prey species. Early research on this topic emphasized how difficult it is for wolves to catch healthy ungulates. Later research, much of it done in Alaska, documents ways that predators sometimes limit ungulate populations, often by preying heavily on young ungulates. Research on these issues is often complicated by other factors, such as geography, climate, the species composition of the predator-prey system, the presence of multiple predators, and human predation.

In general, wolves cannot kill whenever and whatever they choose. They traverse large territories and hunt strenuously to find enough food to sustain themselves. It has to be that way. Any predator capable of killing at will would destroy its own food supply and become a footnote in evolutionary history. For a predator-prey system to work, there must be parity between the eater and the eaten.

And that is the case. Deer are usually too alert to be stalked or too quick to be caught. Moose and elk might outrun wolves or might stand them off with deadly flailing hooves. Caribou, even young calves, can usually outrun wolves.

Yet wolves survive. One way they persevere is by traveling so many miles that they sooner or later cross paths with a vulnerable animal. That is the main reason wolf territories are so large. Putting it the other way around, wolves wouldn't range so far if it were easy for them to kill all the animals living in their vicinity.

Prey animals become vulnerable in a number of ways. Some suffer from arthritis, disease, parasites, or injury. Some individuals are a little less wary, a little slower to flee, a little indecisive when challenged. The very old and very young are especially vulnerable.

Sometimes an exceptionally harsh winter makes groups of ungulates too weak to escape. Under those circumstances, wolves sometimes engage in "spree" killing. If wolves encounter several nearly starved deer trapped in a winter yarding area, they might kill all or most of them in one bloody binge, dining on the choice parts and leaving the rest. This kind of feeding is not typical, yet it occurs.

All this does not mean wolves are incapable of catching healthy animals. Sometimes they can, although the odds favor the prey unless it is compromised in some way. Wolves cannot afford to waste energy chasing healthy animals. Prey animals, for their part, have various ways of indicating to wolves that they are too healthy to be caught, as we'll see in a moment.

Many prey animals killed by wolves would have died of something else if the wolves had not come along when they did. When researchers examine wolf kills, they find that a remarkably high percentage of the victims have skeletal deformities, injuries, or unhealthy bone marrow. These animals were in deep trouble before the wolves found them. By weeding out the sick and unfit animals, wolves benefit the healthy ones. Now that chronic wasting disease (CWD) is threatening elk in the Rocky Mountain states, some people who feared wolves would decimate elk are beginning to wonder if wolves could possibly benefit elk populations by removing sick individuals before they pass the disease along to others. If this happens, it has not yet been documented, but such beneficial culling is part of the logic of the overall predator-prey relationship. Predators often do remove unfit individuals from an ungulate population before they have passed along their disease or defective genes to future generations.

Almost always, the prey that wolves can catch is compromised by being sick, young, aged, or injured in some way.

Predator and prey populations exist in balance, but that balance is not as simple as many think.

The concept of "balance of nature" is widely misunderstood. The basic idea is that predator and prey species must exist in equilibrium. Wolves control deer numbers by preying on the weakest and least fit individuals; deer control wolf numbers by being difficult to catch, thus limiting the amount of food available to wolves.

This balance is more complicated than most people picture it. People often assume that wolves control ungulate populations by the total numbers they kill, yet the real controlling factor is usually the productivity of the land and fluctuations in the climate. A harsh winter might reduce moose or deer numbers, and that in turn affects wolf numbers. Weather fluctuations, rising and falling ungulate populations, rising and falling wolf numbers, and the basic health of the browse that sustains the ungulates all are constantly changing and affecting each other.

The notion of "balance" in the balance of nature is also more complex than many people think. In any particular predator-prey system at any moment in time, it is not only possible but probable that the balance may not match the theoretical idea. That is, there will usually be too many predators or too many ungulates. This balance is dynamic, not static, and it is best understood when viewed in terms of average populations over many decades, not just a year or two.

The hunt

A wolf on the move is probably always hungry and probably always hunting. And wolves are on the move about eight hours of every day. Sometimes pack members trot along in single file, particularly when hunting in deep snow. At other times, they fan out to cover more ground and improve the odds of flushing out a potential meal.

Sooner or later, a pack member sees or smells an animal that might be prey. The pack then becomes excited, although each wolf exercises restraint, moving forward in silence. Wolves learn they must be close to prey before they can launch a successful charge. And wolves know better than to howl when stalking prey.

The most dramatic moment in the hunt occurs when prey and predator make eye contact. Wolves learn much by studying the response of their intended prey. Healthy, self-confident animals might flee or make a stand. Weak ungulates cannot help giving off signals that betray the fact they are vulnerable. Somehow, wolves can discriminate between the moose that stands its ground because it doesn't trust itself to run and the moose that stands its ground because it doesn't feel the need to run.

Author Barry Lopez has written somewhat romantically about the moment when predator and prey study each other. Lopez calls this the "conversation of death." In effect, the wolves are asking the ungulate, "Are you ready to die today?" The reply of a vigorous animal is, "Hell no!" But some individuals cannot manage such a firm denial. Their body language betrays their weakness, fear, and confusion. Then the wolves press the issue. Lopez goes so far as to say these weak individuals give permission to take their lives.

Scientists are more comfortable speaking of what they call a "testing" process. Testing often involves harassing prey animals to make them run. Injured, weak, or panicky animals show their vulnerability in the way they move. Wolves have an uncanny ability to detect the one caribou in a sea of stampeding caribou that isn't running as fluidly as the rest, and once they lock in on a weak animal they never seem to lose their focus.

Lopez's "conversation of death" helps explain some cases of livestock depredation. Wolves sometimes run amok among livestock, slaughtering more animals than they possibly could eat. Centuries of domestication have turned livestock animals – which were once wild species – into dependent idiots with few natural instincts. When wolves challenge them, sheep and cattle panic, exhibiting exactly those signals that unfit wild animals display.

Researcher Dan MacNulty recently made a fascinating observation on wolf-elk interactions at Yellowstone. After studying hours of film showing wolves testing elk, MacNulty realized elk have a way of telling wolves that they are too fit to be killed. Healthy elk, when tested by wolves, adopt a highly stylized way of trotting, lifting their hooves high and holding their heads back. It is a highly *inefficient* way of running that reeks of showboating, and that is exactly the point. These elk are saying, in effect, "I'm so strong I can run in this stupid way, and you'll still never catch me!" Compromised elk cannot or do not use that stylized trot. They hold their heads low and just try to blend in with the herd, which is surely one thing wolves learn to spot.

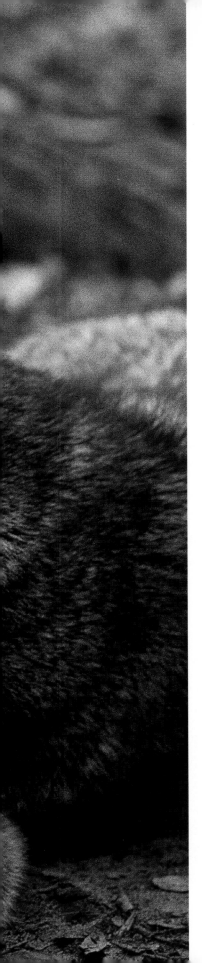

CHAPTER 8

The Enigmatic Red Wolf

In 1624, eight years after his life was saved by Pocahontas, Captain John Smith published *A General History of Virginia*. In it, he noted, "The wolves are not much bigger than our English fox." Smith was the first European to describe the red wolf (*Canis rufus*), the enigmatic wild canid of the eastern seaboard and the southeastern US. He didn't seem to doubt it was a wolf.

Other people have. Nothing about the red wolf has caused so much scientific confusion as its identity and derivation. Is it a wolf? If so, is it a subspecies of the gray wolf? Might it just be a gray wolf-coyote hybrid? Or could it possibly be the sole survivor of a primitive race of wolves? Or, however it derived, is the red wolf the same species as the wolf of southeastern Canada?

These are not esoteric questions.

If you are a biologist dedicated to saving the last red wolves on earth, you fret about these issues because you need to decide which of the animals in the recovery zone are wolf-coyote hybrids and which are true red wolves. If the animal you are handling is a hybrid, you must destroy or sterilize it; if the animal is a true red wolf, you need to protect it and do anything to help it survive.

If you are a lawyer for the American sheep producers, you argue in court that the US Fish and Wildlife Service (USFWS) should not restore the red wolf as an endangered species because it isn't a *species*, but a hybrid.

If you are a USFWS manager, the issue is nettlesome because your agency isn't supposed to promote the spread of hybrids.

The red wolf looks like a leggy German shepherd with a short coat, noticeably prominent ears, and a long, narrow muzzle. The coat is often a lovely copper or cinnamon color, frequently mixed with gray or black. Early naturalists spoke of a black Florida wolf, which might have been a black color phase of the red wolf. Whatever it was, that wolf is now gone.

Debate about the true nature of the red wolf shows no signs of going away. Early arguments were based on the relatively crude process of analyzing skeletal remains. Recent studies have employed the powerful tool of DNA analysis. But the furor over the real nature of the red wolf demonstrates the limitations of DNA evidence, for taxonomists

Red wolf managers pioneered many techniques later used on gray wolves.

still can't agree if the red wolf is essentially a hybrid or a distinct subtype of wolf.

There are several theories. At one time, scientists speculated that red wolves might have been the original wolf in America, but more recent analyses have cast doubt on that theory. A more recent hypothesis holds that red wolves, gray wolves, and coyotes all derived from a common ancestor. The gray wolf, it is thought, migrated to Europe and Asia, developed into its modern form there, and later reappeared on the North American continent. In this view, the red wolf we know today is an old mixture of early gray wolf, coyote, and ancient red wolf.

Recently, some taxonomists have suggested that the red wolf as virtually identical to *Canis lupus lycaon*, the delicate wolves of southeastern Canada most famously associated with Ontario's Algonquin Park. They look remarkably similar, and the similarities extend to much shared genetic material. Taxonomists want to call this animal the "eastern Canadian wolf." If the red wolf and the little wolf of southeastern Canada are the same, this animal once ranged all the way from Texas to southeastern Canada, roughly a third of the continent.

What everyone agrees upon is ultimately more important than what remains in dispute. All taxonomists agree on two points. Whatever the red wolf is, it has been around for a very long time – estimates run between 13,000 and

300,000 years – and it was the top canid predator of the eastern seaboard. Second, everyone agrees that whatever the red wolf is, it is *the* legitimate wolf of the eastern US, a highly endangered animal that deserves every effort required to protect and restore it.

It would be wonderful to confirm that the red wolf and the wolf of southeastern Canada are the same animal. In that case, red wolves would not be nearly as endangered as previously thought. That would mean that a wealth of genetic diversity is available to ensure that red wolves continue to be viable, because all of today's red wolves derive from a genetic base of just 14 animals. But if these two wolves are not precisely the same species, to mix their genes now would be to destroy the uniqueness of the red wolf. For that reason, red wolf managers are proceeding cautiously while taxonomists quarrel about the status of these similar-looking wolves.

Red wolves are tracked by telemetry that reveals their location and signals if they have not moved in some time – signs mishap or mortality.

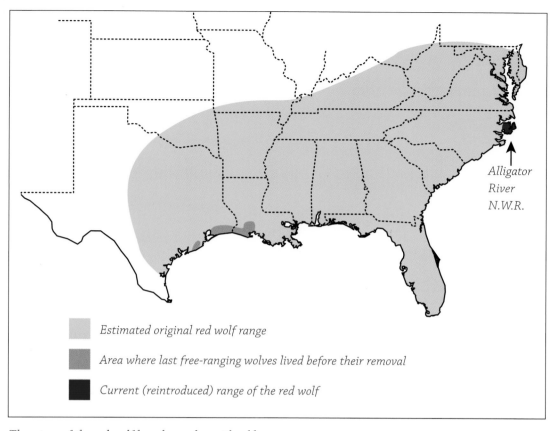

Estimated original red wolf range

Area where last free-ranging wolves lived before their removal

Current (reintroduced) range of the red wolf

Alligator River N.W.R.

The range of the red wolf has changed considerably.

All of this reflects the fact that "species" is not a hard-edged and clear concept. An animal species can develop in any number of ways, including through ancient hybridization. And "species" is a slippery term when used in the world of canids, anyway, for wolves, dogs, and coyotes can interbreed and produce viable offspring.

A 1992 symposium of biologists determined that the red wolf is an important and critically threatened animal deserving of every protection. In the words of Curtis Carley, a founder of the red wolf recovery program, "Whatever the red wolf is, the wolves we have . . . seem to breed true and represent the southeastern canine that has been recorded as part of our past." Any animal that has been a keystone species in an ecosystem for hundreds of thousand years has a strong presumptive case for belonging in that ecosystem.

The red wolf

The red wolf once ranged over much of the southeastern quarter of the US. It lived as far west as central Texas and as far north as Illinois (unless it is the same as the wolf of southeastern Canada, which would vastly increase its northern range). It was the top canine predator of southeastern forests, occupying the niche filled by coyotes in the desert west and gray wolves in the north.

Little is known about the habits of red wolves in the wild. By the time scientists began taking a serious interest in red wolves in the 1960s, it was too late to conduct field studies. The few remaining wolves were struggling to survive in wretched, atypical habitat. Their social structure had been warped by the twin stresses of persecution and severely depressed population levels. Much of what biologists now know about red wolves comes from the

A technician works with an anesthetized red wolf, assessing its health.

first few generations of wolves reintroduced into the wild.

Because the first field studies of red wolves were done on animals occupying marginal habitat, biologists thought they mainly preyed on medium-sized mammals such as nutria and raccoons. And when red wolves were first reintroduced to the wild, they did prey heavily on raccoons. Since then, they have shown proficiency at taking whitetail deer. The wolves of Algonquin Park, supposing they are the same

animal, even take down moose.

Studies on the first wolves reintroduced to the wild have yielded much information. Some researchers had speculated that red wolves would live in small family groups like coyotes, but the wolves have proven to be more social than expected. Two-year-old red wolves frequently behave like young gray wolves, remaining with their parents in packs to hunt, defend territory, and help raise the pups. The first reintroduced red wolves are defending territories of 20 to over 100 square miles (52 to over 259 km²). Red wolves are often described as more furtive and nocturnal than gray wolves.

The drift toward extinction

These shy little wolves suffered the same fate as wolves elsewhere when Europeans began remaking the face of the wolves' land. Settlers razed forests and put the land to other uses. When unregulated hunting virtually eliminated whitetail deer, wolves preyed on sheep and cattle. People retaliated. Wolves were shot, trapped, and poisoned until, in 1980, the species was declared extinct in the wild.

In the late 1960s, the red wolf made its last stand in 1,700 square miles (4,400 km²) of pestilent, sodden marshland in the shadow of giant petrochemical facilities along the coast of Texas and Louisiana. This was vile wolf habitat. Wolves died from mange, hookworm, and heartworm. Mosquito populations were so high that calves in the area sometimes smothered from all the insects packed in their nostrils.

Things seemed hopeless for the remaining few red wolves when Texas biology professor Howard McCarley began calling attention to another insidious threat: the last red wolves on earth were hybridizing with coyotes. As wolves were eliminated from the western portions of their range, coyotes expanded their range to occupy the void. Red wolf populations ultimately dropped so low that wolves began mating with coyotes, leading to what biologists call "hybrid swarm," the loss of species integrity through hybridization. The world's population of red wolves was estimated at 100 highly beleaguered animals.

Even before there was a federal law to protect endangered species, biologists were putting red wolves near the top of a list of species thought to be in imminent danger of extinction. The red wolf received that dubious distinction in 1965. Even so, federal programs to eliminate wolves continued to eradicate red wolves for another year.

When the US Congress passed the Endangered Species Act (ESA) of 1973, the red wolf was one of the first species listed. The USFWS had already established a recovery program, mainly based on protecting the last red wolves by killing all coyotes in a "buffer zone" around the last scrap of wolf habitat.

The plan flopped. Trappers kept catching animals that they could not positively identify as true wolves or wolf-coyote hybrids. Any animal suspected of having coyote blood had to be destroyed. It was a gut-wrenching process because managers suspected they were euthanizing some true red wolves at a time when they were among the most endangered species in the world.

Managers ultimately decided to do the most desperate thing imaginable. They removed all remaining red wolves from the wild. Since they couldn't protect red wolves in the wild, they would protect them in zoos. This seemed to defy the ESA, which specifically charged the USFWS with saving endangered species in the wild. Managers at the time knew they might be making a terrible mistake. One said, "We weren't sure if we wouldn't be blamed for the extermination of the red wolf." Placing the last red wolves on Earth in zoo cages reminded some of the notorious statement from the Vietnam War: "We had to destroy the village in order to save it."

US government trappers collected over 400 wild canids, examined them, and sent the presumptive wolves – just 43 animals – to a new captive breeding facility in the Port Defiance Zoo in Tacoma, Washington. It was a blessing that Port Defiance was ready to do this work, for no other zoo in the country would lower itself to harbor wolves.

Things went badly at first. Some wolves died. Several were destroyed when it was deemed they might have coyote blood. The number of healthy and genetically true red wolves stood at one time at the frighteningly low number of 14 wolves. And they weren't breeding at first.

But then some did, and slowly their numbers built up until the 14 original animals had grown to over 200 by 1992.

Experimental and nonessential

With that many wolves to work with, biologists began studying where they might be restored to the wild. Managers faced two distinctly different problems: one biological and one political. Nobody knew how to insert a zoo-born predator in wild habitat in such a way that the animal had much of a chance of surviving. And it was clear that the whole program would face stiff public resistance.

That became apparent when public opposition forced managers to give up on their first plan, which was to release red wolves in the Land Between the Lakes region of Kentucky and Tennessee. Livestock and hunting groups organized against the program, and even some environmentalists were not supportive. Managers made the most of a bad situation, learning from their mistakes.

A 1982 amendment to the ESA gave managers an opportunity to try again. This amendment created the option of an "experimental and nonessential" designation. This would allow managers to conduct a species reintroduction without adhering to all the requirements of the original ESA, which were seen by some in the public as rigid and onerous. Under this new designation, troublesome reintroduced wolves could be removed from the wild, an action not allowed by the original ESA. The relaxed designation also made it possible for managers to permit sport hunting in the release area, even if doing so might occasionally result in the death of a wolf.

This new designation was a two-edged sword, offering both advantages and risks. Red wolves would be released into the wild with less legal protection than envisioned under the original ESA. That was a concern, and yet managers feared the worst if they tried to force wolves upon an unwilling local population that often carried guns. The original ESA quickly established a dubious reputation with many groups who believed it was unreasonably restrictive, particularly in its impact on traditional uses of the local landscape, such as hunting.

In one view, the critical decision to use the experimental and nonessential designation became the most important legacy of the red wolf program, because it created a useful precedent later used in other wolf restoration programs. This decision eliminated some of the absolutistic and legalistic qualities of the ESA, making it possible for managers to present themselves as pragmatic, cooperative people, not agents of a rigid government bureaucracy.

Restoration

Where could wolves go? In general, there is very little suitable habitat remaining for wolves. In 1984, an insurance company donated 118,000 acres (47,000 hectares) of swampy land on the coast of North Carolina to the USFWS. By happy coincidence, the Alligator River National Wildlife Refuge (ARNWR) was ideal for red wolf reintroduction. The area was big enough and rich with potential prey. Even better, there were few people, no livestock, and no coyotes present. Because the refuge was a peninsula with water on three sides, managers could monitor and control wolf movements better here than elsewhere. Federal managers later acquired an adjacent parcel of land called the Pocosin Lakes area, offering another 110,000 acres (45,000 hectares) of potential wolf habitat. The experimental population area now includes 1.7 million acres (688,000 hectares).

Four pairs of wolves were released in ARNWR in 1987. It was the first time an extirpated predator had ever been reintroduced to the wild in the US, and possibly the first time in the world.

Because managers rightfully worried about how well a zoo-born predator would adjust to life in the wild, they devised a technique they called a "soft release." Soft release is a commonsensical protocol developed to ease the shock of the transition from zoo cage to the dangers of the natural world. This became the second critical pioneering technique that would later be used by some other wolf reintroductions.

Wolf families were confined in acclimation pens, where they could live in safety long enough to bond with the area and come to regard it as "home." Managers minimized contact with wolves and even treated their highly endangered wolves brusquely to discourage them from developing doglike bonds with hu-

mans. Penned wolves were fed road-killed animals. Wolves were even given live prey so they could practice killing their own food. When the time was right, the pen doors were opened. Red wolves – even if just a few – were once again free to roam and hunt in some of their original habitat.

Learning to be real wolves

The red wolf reintroduction was founded on a rather optimistic supposition. Nobody knew whether an animal born and reared in confinement could learn to become an effective predator capable of killing its own food and

The red wolf continues to stymie taxonomists but is delighting increasing legions of red wolf fans.

avoiding all the threats of life in the wild. The first wolves released would know nothing about the world around them. They would not know how dangerous an alligator or a car could be. They wouldn't know how to find and take down a deer.

In the first decade of the program, 71 captive-born red wolves were released into ARNWR. About 70 percent died shortly after their release – hit by cars, killed by other wolves, drowned, or recaptured when they associated with humans. Some just disappeared. In red wolf releases with known results, only 21 percent of the time did the wolf live long enough for the release to be judged successful.

As discouraging as that might seem, managers familiar with the challenges were not surprised. It is hard enough to be a wolf, and wild-bred wolves die all the time. It was obviously going to be difficult for captive-born an-imals to learn the ways of wolves quickly enough to survive long enough to breed.

As explained by one veteran manager, "When you put zoo-bred animals in the wild, you know many are not going to live. So you dump more wolves out there. And most of them die. And so you dump some more. Finally, a few will beat the odds and survive. They give birth to some pups. And when those wild-born pups give birth, those are *real wolves!*"

And then the magic moment: in 1988, program director Mike Phillips was circling a mated pair – wolves 211M and 196F – when he saw a "small, black ball of fur" hustling to catch up with its parents. This little wolf was the first red wolf to be born in the wild under the new program, the first of many to come.

The numbers of wolves began to build . . . numbers of *real* wolves, the second- and third-generation of wild forebears.

Red wolves have twice narrowly escaped extinction, once from human persecution and once from genetic swamping by coyotes.

Hybridization

The restoration program hit a wall just when it seemed that it had succeeded. From 1994 on, managers became increasingly concerned about the re-emergence of an old problem. Coyotes were mingling with red wolves, breeding, and mixing coyote genes with red wolf genes.

The problem was so serious that some thoughtful observers concluded that the whole red wolf program was doomed.

A major assessment of the program in 1999 produced a new plan for action. The "Adaptive Management Program" was an experimental and aggressive plan born of desperation. Red wolf habitat was divided into three zones. The most eastern area, Zone 1, lay out toward the tip of the peninsula, farthest from all the coyotes living to the west. Zone 2, the middle zone, had some coyotes. Zone 3 lay adjacent to country where coyotes ranged freely, and it originally had many coyotes.

The Adaptive Management Program subjected Zone 1 coyotes and hybrids to a high level of control. All coyotes and wolf-hybrids were killed. When these coyotes and wolf-hybrids were caught in Zone 2, they were sterilized and then released. There was some management of coyotes and hybrids in Zone 3, but it was much less intense than in the prime wolf zones.

All of this required managers to slog countless miles in swamps, monitoring animal movements and trapping coyotes and hybrids. It was extraordinarily difficult, dirty work.

But it paid off. As coyotes and hybrids disappeared from Zone 1, red wolves prospered. Natural dispersal sent more wolves into Zone 2. There they helped defend Zone 2 against coyotes, until gradually the whole management area began to fill with wolves.

The continued success of this plan will depend on continued aggressive removal or sterilization of coyotes and hybrids, but the real threat to the red wolf from hybridization seems to be passing.

Augmenting natural reproduction

Two programs have introduced more wolves and precious genetic diversity to the population.

Wolves are being bred in the wild on two islands, Bull's Island (off the South Carolina shore) and Saint Vincent Island (in the Gulf of Mexico). Each island is home to a breeding pair of red wolves. Pups from those islands are released in the other parts of the red wolf experimental area when they are 18 months old. These island-born wolves have done well because they are cannier about living as wild wolves than captive-bred animals.

The most recent management innovation is called "fostering." In an effort to maximize the number of red wolf pups being raised by wild red wolf mothers, managers remove pups born in captivity and add them to the litters of wild wolves of the same age. Mother wolves readily accept these "foster" offspring and raise them as if they were their own. The captive-bred pups benefit from the education they receive from a wild wolf mother, and they have done very well.

The overall numbers are beginning to look good for the program. There are now about 160 adult red wolves in various captive breeding programs. They produce anywhere from 8 to 25 pups a year. Approximately 100 adult red wolves live in the wild, distributed among 18 to 22 packs. The numbers go up each year. In the spring of 2004, a record number of 56 pups were born. According to Bud Fazio, director of the red wolf restoration program, "The population is becoming very healthy."

Human relations

Antagonism toward the red wolf program and the ESA could have doomed the species early on, but managers have worked hard to educate the public and quickly deal with any incident that could cause trouble for the program. The relaxed experimental and nonessential designation has not imposed onerous restrictions on land use. That may be one reason that few wolves have been killed by humans. Increasingly, as more people hear the unique story of the red wolf and as wolf tourism becomes more prominent, local public opinion supports the presence of the wolves.

Local landowners have been much more supportive of wolf restoration here than elsewhere. A significant number of landowners believe red wolves control nuisance animals such as nutria, which destroy dams, and raccoons, which prey on bobwhite quail and wild turkeys. Much of the credit goes to the wolves themselves. Red wolves have been amazingly well behaved, not going after livestock. Since the first reintroduction in 1977, there are only four "incidents" involving wolves and livestock, all minor.

Good feelings for wolves might increase when they emerge from relative obscurity. A major effort is being made to create a modern red wolf visitor's center. It would serve as an educational facility and a hub for the popular howling programs. Because of the limitations of facilities, many wolf fans are now being turned away.

Nevertheless, this public acceptance of the red wolf program might have been purchased at a high price. Some observers believe the implementation of experimental and nonessential designation might have been overly permissive, making it hard to protect red wolves from being killed illegally. The regulations might need tuning. But it is in the nature of wolf management that changing conditions and changing attitudes constantly require adjustments to management programs.

The future

Make no mistake about it: The red wolf remains a highly endangered animal. With so few red wolves alive and with the ever-present threat of genetic swamping by coyotes, it isn't possible to celebrate anything like a "final" triumph in the effort to restore red wolves.

Moreover, the whole restoration program is limited to a single site (not counting the two offshore breeding islands). As such, red wolf restoration is more of a demonstration project than an overall return of wolves to former habitat such as has taken place with gray wolves in other regions. In the densely settled eastern US, there are no places where more red wolves could be reintroduced without encountering coyotes. If red wolves are to be restored in any new locations, managers will need to sustain a ferocious level of coyote management.

A huge question mark hanging over today's red wolf program is uncertainty over the relationship between red wolves and the Canadian wolves associated with Ontario's Algonquin Park. The current program rests on a narrow genetic base of 14 original animals. If some of Algonquin's wolves could be added to the gene pool of the red wolf program, the program would suddenly gain health dramatically.

The red wolf has benefited enormously from the creative contributions of the Red Wolf Coalition, a private group that has followed innovative programs for developing public support for this highly endangered wolf. This is particularly important since the red wolf recovery area includes so much private land. The coalition sponsors red wolf education programs, including a Hunter Outreach Program. The group conducts popular public "howlings." A priority for the coalition now is raising funds to build the Red Wolf Center in wolf country in Tyrrell County. The facility would be an educational and interpretive center where visitors can learn about red wolves and view a captive pack in natural habitat. Additionally, the coalition works closely with other organizations including the North Carolina Zoo to foster interest in red wolves.

No matter what happens to the USFWS red wolf program in the future, it has already accomplished a great deal. The red wolf is the first predator ever to be restored to the wild after becoming effectively extinct. The red wolf program pioneered the relaxed protocol of the experimental and nonessential designa-

Red wolf restoration will always be geographically limited, but it seems headed for success after some great difficulties.

tion. The soft release was invented here, as was the technique of fostering. The effort to restore gray wolves owes a huge debt to the innovative work of red wolf managers.

The researchers and managers of this program have come a very long way, traveling mostly without any kind of map. More challenges must be overcome if they are to meet the ambitious long-term goals of the program of establishing a population of 220 wolves in the wild.

The red wolf program tested two great questions whose answers were very much in doubt. The first was whether a zoo-reared wolf would be too compromised by its limited upbringing to ever succeed in the wild. Most wolves failed that terrible test, but enough succeeded to bring the whole program to its present level. The second question was whether humans could tolerate the close presence of red wolves, a "new" predator to them.

It would be impossible to say which challenge was the more daunting. So far, both people and wolves have behaved better than almost anyone would have predicted. The dramatic – if limited – comeback of the red wolf is a major triumph of modern wildlife management.

CHAPTER 9

Wolves of the
Western Great Lakes

Although scientists want us to call these animals "gray wolves," everyone who is not a scientist calls them "timber wolves." The subspecies of gray wolf found in Minnesota, Wisconsin, and Michigan in the US is *Canis lupus nubilis,* the Great Plains wolf. Taxonomists formerly thought the wolf of these states was the eastern timber wolf, *Canis lupus lycaon,* but now agree it has always been *nubilis.*

The *nubilis* subtype is typical of gray wolves everywhere – typical in size, appearance, and habits. These wolves range in size from 50 to 100 pounds (23 to 46 kg), averaging about 70 pounds (32 kg). Most have coats that are a mix of gray, black, and tan, although some wolves in the region are a light cream color and a few are black. Most packs have four to six wolves.

Wolves here are highly associated with the upper third of these states, lands whose beguiling mix of lakes and coniferous forests have attracted vacationers for decades. Yet wolves were once more numerous on the southern prairies where herds of elk, bison, antelope, and deer grazed. Because of unimpeded sightlines, prairie wildlife was easy for market hunters to exploit. Large ungulates and the wolves that fed on them disappeared from prairie once trains made travel to the region easy. By the first decades of the 20th century, all remaining wolves lived in the coniferous forests of the northern regions of these states.

Originally, the northern forests of these states featured towering stands of white pines. When 19th century lumberjacks felled and removed the great pines, what grew up on the cleared land was a brushier forest featuring such trees as aspen, maple, and birch. What had been caribou and moose habitat became superb deer habitat. Deer and wolves flourished in these second-growth forests in the early decades of the 20th century, until some forests began to age by the middle of the century.

Wolf eradication never became an all-out war in this region, as it did in the western US. The west was dominated by the livestock industry. Cattle ranchers and sheepherders agreed on almost nothing except that both hated wolves, so the whole society was committed to wolf extermination. The lands around the western Great Lakes, on the other hand, had mixed economies. The mining, tourism, and logging industries had no special reason to kill wolves.

Even so, wolves were considered vermin that should be eliminated. Bounties – some of them remarkably generous – hastened the process. When the first Michigan state legislature met in 1838, almost the first bill it passed established a bounty on wolves. Wolves were killed for their luxurious pelts and because they were considered a menace, but mainly because people assumed that wiping out wolves would boost deer numbers. Deer were popular as a source of food and as the animal that made cash registers ring during hunting season. Unlike wolves, deer had economic value.

When Wisconsin deer numbers plummeted in the 1940s, biologist Bill Feeney organized a team of biologists to study the problem. Feeney determined that the deer herd was starving because it had badly overgrazed its range. But he also knew that the public blamed wolves for the decline in deer. So skittish was Feeney about hostility toward wolves that he kept his pioneering research a secret, never even revealing its results to fellow scientists.

By 1965, wolves had been extirpated from 97 percent of their original range in the Lower 48 states of the US. Nobody has ever ventured to estimate the original population of wolves in the US, but it would have been a stunning number, probably several million. That had been reduced to about 700 wolves in northeastern Minnesota, plus a handful on Isle Royale. Those Minnesota wolves survived the great extirpation primarily because of the Superior National Forest, an immense wilderness area stretching along 150 miles (241 km) of border with Ontario. Ontario has a wilderness area of the same size on its side of the border, including Quetico Park. Wolf eradication was difficult in northeastern Minnesota because travel was so difficult there and because dispersers from Ontario kept replacing the wolves killed on the Minnesota side of the border.

Even so, the wolf seemed doomed in the US.

Then in 1967, just before animal control agents could wipe out the last wolves in North America, the gray wolf went on the endangered species list. The US government assumed responsibility for wolf management, taking it away from the states. With whiplash abruptness, the official status of wolves changed from vermin to persecuted endangered animals, and public policy changed from wolf eradication to wolf restoration.

The recovery plan

Putting an animal on the endangered species list triggers a chain of events. Typically, the US government, through its Fish and Wildlife Service (USFWS), assumes control of that species. Specialists draft a recovery plan to restore the species to some degree of viability in portions of its former range. The law is robust, partly because it is designed to prevent species extinction, which is an environmental tragedy.

In the case of the gray wolf, in 1978 a team of managers drafted a plan for gray wolf recovery in the western Great Lakes states. The plan was tweaked in 1992; in 2003 it was modified further to include a broader geographic region called the Eastern Distinct Population Segment (the Eastern DPS; see page 33).

The recovery team's first priority was to build the strength of wolf populations in Minnesota. Managers believed wolves would prosper if they were just given a break from human persecution. In view of the natural fertility and footloose ways of wolves, the team expected wolves to build numbers and expand their range without the aid of expensive translocations or habitat projects.

As the team knew, there had been one earlier attempt to translocate wolves. In 1974, four Minnesota wolves were released in Michigan's Marquette County. Within a year, all four were dead, killed by humans or their vehicles.

A recovery plan includes numerical goals that define success for the plan. Experts analyzed wolf habitat in the three states and estimated how many wolves might live there. For wolves to be officially recovered in this region, the team wanted to see a minimum population in Minnesota of 1,251 to 1,400 wolves. For greater stability, the team also wanted a second viable population of at least 100 wolves outside of Minnesota but nearby. That population was expected to appear in northern Wisconsin and the Upper Peninsula of Michigan. The team specified that when all those minimum goals were met for five successive years, the gray wolf would be officially recovered in the region.

Wolves initially enjoyed total protection. As an endangered species, the gray wolf could not be killed by anyone, even if it preyed on livestock. In 1978, Minnesota wolves were reclassified as a threatened species, allowing authorized agents to remove wolves that attacked pets or livestock. The same process happened somewhat later in Wisconsin and Michigan as their wolf numbers rebounded. Some folks still killed wolves illegally when the opportunity appeared, but those losses weren't high enough to affect wolf restoration. And with passing time, more people accepted the new view of wolves as legitimate and valued members of northern ecosystems.

Minnesota

In 1964, anyone who killed a wolf in northern Minnesota was a local hero who could claim a bounty equivalent to over $200 in today's currency. Just a few years later, anyone killing a wolf was a poacher who faced a stiff fine and possible jail time. But public law changed far faster than public attitudes could. Northern Minnesotans resented what they saw as an unwarranted intrusion into local affairs by a fed-

Minnesota wolves have rebounded vigorously.

eral bureaucracy. People found various ways of registering their protest, and more than a few wolves paid a price for the hostility some citizens felt toward the government.

One prerequisite for wolf restoration is a strong base of prey animals. That did not exist at first in Minnesota. Aging habitat and a series of harsh winters put the deer herd in trouble. Things were so desperate in 1971 that the Minnesota Department of Natural Resources (DNR) cancelled the hunting season. That crisis gave birth to a far more sophisticated deer management program.

A revolution in logging also helped. Loggers had disregarded aspen, considering it a "junk tree" with no commercial value. Then the wood products industry developed commercially viable ways to use aspen. There was a sudden surge of logging in the many large stands of aspen. Dense young forests shot up after aspen stands were clear-cut, and these were superb deer habitat. Responding to ideal habitat, easy winters, and better deer management, the Minnesota deer herd built to record levels in the early 1990s.

The booming deer herd helped wolves in two ways. All that venison was the fuel needed to drive a rapidly expanding wolf population. Just as important, anti-wolf spokesmen who predicted wolves would "wipe out" Minnesota's deer lost all credibility. At the same time as the Minnesota wolf population was booming, state hunters were enjoying record deer harvests. It was obviously possible for Minnesotans to enjoy excellent deer hunting and strong wolf populations at the same time.

Wolf restoration depends on people tolerating wolves. A symbolic turning point in wolf toleration came in 1983, when the Science Museum of Minnesota mounted its exhibit, "Wolves and Men." The show presented the tragic history of wolf persecution in compelling detail.

The exhibit has educated close to three million people to date and continues to be a powerful, popular attraction, now housed at the In-

ternational Wolf Center, in Ely, Minnesota.

There were other indications of new thinking about wolves. Ely, Minnesota now prides itself as host to the International Wolf Center educational facility. Wolves were seen as something positive, not negative. Increasingly, Minnesotans viewed wolves as the victims of irrational persecution, not as threats. It didn't happen right away, but wolf hatred began to give way to wolf acceptance – even wolf adoration.

The history of one pack exemplifies the overall recovery story. From 1969 to 1980, researchers monitored a wolf pack that defended a territory of 100 square miles near the town of Hill City. Dispersers from that pack helped start up five neighboring packs. Wolves from the Hill City pack joined or formed other packs as far as 135 miles (217 km) away.

Minnesota wolf numbers built from several hundred to about 1,200 by the mid-1970s. A survey in the winter of 1988-89 found 1,500 to 1,750 wolves. Nine years later, a comprehensive survey put the number at 2,450 wolves. Wolves had expanded their range to include almost half of the state. Wolf country in Minnesota is now everything to the east of a line from Pine City to Warroad.

It took Minnesota wolves just three decades to saturate empty habitat and reach population levels twice the minimums of the recovery plan. While enforcement – or the threat of enforcement – might have deterred some folks from killing wolves, the dramatic success of wolves was accomplished mainly by dramatically different attitudes toward wolves.

Experts predicted that wolves would continue to increase in numbers and expand their range, but that hasn't happened. A recent survey is currently being analyzed. When published, it will show that Minnesota's wolf population has stabilized or gone down slightly, and the wolf range is the same as when last surveyed. Why?

There are two theories. Wolves are susceptible to outbreaks of sarcoptic mange, a condi-

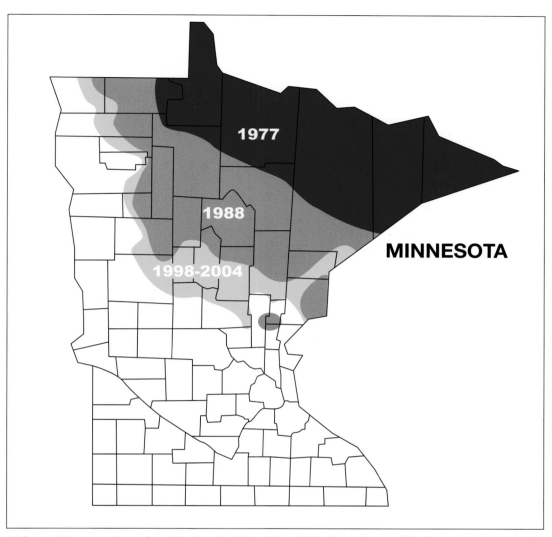

Wolves in Minnesota have thrived under the ESA, although they haven't expanded their range or increased in numbers since 1984.

tion brought on by a mite that causes wolves, foxes, and coyotes to lose hair. Mange is highly contagious, often leading to a slow, agonizing death. Mange has erupted in Minnesota wolf country, and it could be the reason wolves have not expanded in range or numbers in five years. Wolves might also be encountering parvovirus, a disease of dogs. As wolves live closer to humans, they increasingly are at risk from the diseases of people's pets.

A second difficulty has been a succession of mild winters. Minnesota has experienced so many mild winters in recent years that people wonder if this is an impact of global warming. Mild winters favor deer and work against wolves. When deer are not limited by deep snows or stressed by extreme cold, they eat well, travel freely, and remain frisky all winter long. That's good for them, bad for wolves. Wolves thrive on winter-weakened deer.

The biggest surprise is how well wolves and people have been coexisting. Wolf experts once assumed wolves could not exist outside wilderness. But wolves have shown an unexpected readiness to live near people. Researcher Sam Merrill was amazed to discover wolves in a National Guard training area. And while the area has a great many deer, it is anything but wilderness. Abrams tanks rumble within yards of denning wolves. When 155-millimeter Howitzers open up in practice, the wolves often walk toward the booming just to check out the source of the racket. Wolves seem to have no trouble distinguishing between noisy war games and violence directed *toward them*.

A recent study concluded that Minnesota could comfortably accommodate about 2,000 wolves. The current count is 500 wolves over that number. If wolves begin building numbers again, the next 500 or 1,000 wolves are going to show up in places where they are highly likely to cause trouble.

Wisconsin

Wisconsin adopted a wolf bounty while the US Civil War was still being fought. By 1900, wolves had been extirpated from the lower two-thirds of the state. Wolves were harder to find and kill in the thick timber of Wisconsin's northern counties, yet generous bounties inspired plenty of people to try. Hunters' successes took their toll, reducing numbers relentlessly.

And then there was one. The last Wisconsin survivor was Old Two Toes of Bayfield County, a legendary wolf that managed to elude bullets and traps for years. When a banker driving in a whirling snowstorm saw the old wolf trotting on a county highway, he struck him with his car. Old Two Toes didn't die easily. The banker twice pummeled the wolf's head with a tire iron and then had to finish him off by slitting his throat. The carcass was sent to Madison where it could be preserved as a memento of pioneer days in Wisconsin. It never occurred to anyone that wolves would return to Wisconsin. The wolf was officially declared extinct in Wisconsin in 1960.

Most Wisconsin wolves live in the north, with another group in the central hardwoods.

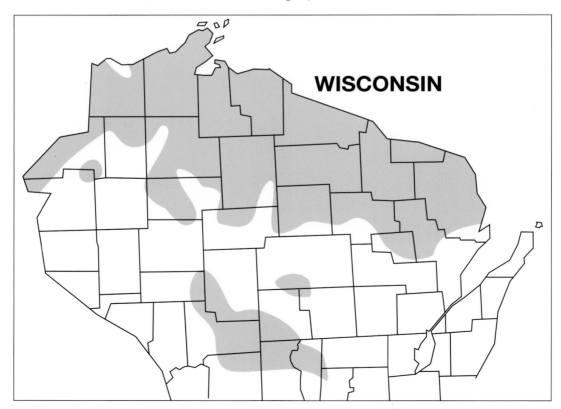

In 1975, the gray wolf was declared endangered in Wisconsin. The recovery plan for Wisconsin was simple. Wisconsin managers had to wait for Minnesota's wolf numbers to build until some dispersers found their way to all the empty habitat and deer awaiting them in northern Wisconsin.

That began to happen in the mid-1970s. Minnesota's Nemadji State Forest, a lightly used area with thick brush, lies south of Duluth and Superior along the Minnesota-Wisconsin border. A pack of wolves set up housekeeping there and began hunting back and forth across the state border. Dispersers from the Stateline Flowage pack soon trotted east. By 1980, Wisconsin had five active packs.

Wolf restoration didn't happen overnight. In the early days of the program, many wolves were shot or struck by cars. But populations began to build in a steadily increasing way that made researchers optimistic.

Then, in the mid-1980s, the recovery hit a wall. For several years almost no pups survived. Managers suspected canine parvovirus. Wolves occasionally contract such canine maladies as distemper, Lyme disease, parvo, heartworm, mange, and rabies. But wolves are hardy. After a few years of heartbreaking pup losses, overall numbers began going up again. By 1998, the state's wolf count stood at 180 wolves in 47 packs, well over the recovery goals.

A comprehensive survey in the winter of 2003-2004 found a total of 374 to 410 wolves in 109 packs. Most of Wisconsin's wolves live in the forests of the northern two tiers of counties, with an additional group of 60 wolves living in a separate population in the central forestland centered in Jackson County.

An early issue with Wisconsin wolf managers was highway development. Research suggested roads were a threat to wolves in two ways. Wolves are vulnerable to being hit by vehicles on roads. Roads also open territory to humans, increasing the opportunities for poaching. Many plans for restoration emphasized the absence of roads, since that was considered as necessary as abundant prey for wolves.

Concern about roads diminished when later research showed how casually wolves accepted roads, often making use of them to travel or hunt. Moreover, people were not taking advantage of chances to shoot wolves the way they had early in the restoration program. In the 1980s, 60 percent of all mortality on radio-collared wolves was death by gunshot. That figure is now down as low as 25 percent. This is one of those statistics that might look like "just a number," yet it reflects a stunning change in social perception of wolves. People are accepting wolves, so highways are less of a threat to them. Mortality among adult wolves from all causes was 38 percent in the early 1980s, a level at which wolf populations can barely hold even. It has dropped to 20 percent lately.

The impact of wolves on the Wisconsin deer population has always been controversial. Wisconsin deer hunters have a tradition of blaming wolves for excessive predation on deer, but that hardly seems appropriate now. Wisconsin's deer herd numbers over 1.7 million, which is too much of a good thing. Out of 135 deer-management units in the state, 92 have more deer than the habitat can continue to carry. Managers have developed new hunting regulations designed to harvest does and bring deer numbers back in line with what the habitat will carry.

What is wrong with having so many deer? Unhealthily high deer populations can overbrowse their own habitat, causing long-term damage. Dense deer populations are vulnerable to diseases. Deer become dangerous nuisances when they cross highways.

Since Wisconsin has close to 400 wolves and yet northern deer populations are dangerously high, wolves are obviously not ravaging the deer herd. Each wolf consumes 15 to 18 deer a year, many of those being sick or injured animals that were doomed to die soon anyway.

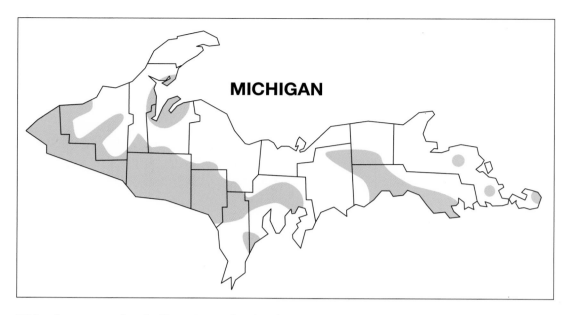

Wolves have returned to the Upper Peninsula of Michigan in strong fashion and now are beginning to show up in the Lower Peninsula, too.

The total number of deer taken by wolves – about 7,000 – is dwarfed by the 450,000 taken by hunters and 40,000 killed each year by cars.

Managers now believe Wisconsin has about as many wolves as it can comfortably absorb, although the "yardstick" of human toleration for wolves seems to be made of rubber. In the 1990s, the population expanded by 20 percent each year. Recently the growth has been just 7 percent. Researchers once calculated that the state had enough habitat for 500 wolves. They currently believe the ideal number might be closer to 350, both in terms of how much suitable wolf habitat the state has and in terms of how many wolves the public will accept.

Having filled the prime habitat, Wisconsin wolves are showing up in odd places. A Wisconsin wolf was killed on a highway near the Fox River Shopping Mall in Appleton. Another died under the wheels of a truck on Interstate Highway 94 east of Madison. One young wolf dispersed to Eastern Indiana. He ended up just short of Ohio, a trip of at least 420 miles (676 km), somehow managing to skirt Chicago without being seen.

The steadily increasing number of depreda-

tion reports might be more evidence of the fact that wolves have filled the best habitat and are now moving into areas where they are likely to get into trouble. In the early years of restoration, wolves stuck to dense forests and ate deer. Now dispersers are traveling through settled areas, encountering more livestock and pets. More farms are suffering livestock losses. Wolves sometimes kill dogs, apparently viewing them as competitors. In one particularly bad year, 17 dogs were lost to wolves, many of them the dogs of bear hunters. Wolves dispersing into settled areas are usually young, less experienced animals, and they are more likely to get into trouble.

The appearance of chronic wasting disease (CWD) in Wisconsin deer has possibly altered the argument. Managers do not currently have data to prove that wolves selectively target deer with CWD, but that seems probable. Deer can live years with the disease before succumbing to it. Wolves have an uncanny ability to sense something subtly amiss in prey animals, so it seems highly likely that wolves would consume sick deer, possibly before those deer pass their disease along to other deer. In the fight to contain CWD, according to wolf manager Adrian Wydeven, "The wolf might be the deer hunter's first line of defense."

The return of wolves to Wisconsin has been a happy story up until now, but the honeymoon could be over. Wolves behaved themselves and didn't attract much attention while they were recolonizing empty habitat. Now they are showing up more often in places where they don't have much of a chance of keeping out of trouble. Wolf hatred used to rest on silly myths and fears, but increasingly wolves are making enemies by preying on livestock or killing beloved pets. The challenge for managers in the coming years will be to preserve strong wolf populations while minimizing conflict with humans.

Michigan

Michigan had a wolf bounty in place before it was a state. In 1817, the US Congress instituted a bounty in what was then called the Northwest Territories, including present Michigan. By 1956, wolves had been extirpated from the Lower Peninsula and only about 100 survivors hung on in the Upper Peninsula. Wolves might have never been completely absent from the state, although in 1974 the population was estimated at just six.

As we have seen, an abortive effort was made to augment the population in 1974, when four wolves from Minnesota were released in Marquette County. They didn't live a year, and the experiment was not repeated.

To restore Michigan's wolf population, the federal recovery team had the same plan it had for Wisconsin. Michigan's abundant wolf habitat would be filled when Minnesota and then Wisconsin wolves grew healthy enough to begin sending dispersers eastward. That began to happen in the early 1970s. A few wolves even might have migrated into the Upper Peninsula (UP) from Ontario in spite of an absence of good travel corridors.

In the spring of 1991, Jim Hammill, Michigan's wolf biologist, confirmed the presence of a denning pack. This was the first time wolves had been known to den in the UP in three decades, although a stray wolf was found hit by a car from time to time.

As happened in other Great Lakes states, numbers began to build. The overall count in 1991 was 17 wolves. Thanks to strong reproductive success and an absence of disease, wolf numbers were estimated at 80 in 1995.

Unfortunately the next winter, the winter of 1995-1996, was exceptionally severe. Weakened by deep snows and cold temperatures, deer suffered heavy losses to wolves. That might account for the fact that wolf numbers declined slightly in the next survey, which showed only 116 wolves. Researchers also noted some occurrence of mange. With few deer to feed upon in the snowy winter of 1997-1998, many wolves died. But wolves rebounded in the next years.

The most recent survey, for the winter of 2003-2004, found 360 wolves in 77 packs. That means Michigan's UP has almost as many wolves as the whole state of Wisconsin. The increase over the previous survey, 12 percent, is healthy, suggesting wolves are not yet saturating the available habitat.

While some deer hunting groups worry about wolves, UP deer hunters haven't raised determined opposition to wolves. Deer numbers are generally good in the UP. The deer herd is not as universally strong as in Minnesota and Wisconsin, but wolves are not the reason. Some counties have more deer than the habitat can support, while others – particularly those that catch a lot of "lake-effect" snow – are never going to have as many deer as counties with mild winters. Wolves kill about 8,000 deer from a population estimated at over 400,000 each year in the UP. That's about two percent for the wolves, but many modern deer hunters don't mind sharing the resource with wolves. The enlightened attitudes of so many deer hunters is one of the most pleasant surprises in the story of the return of the wolf.

The future of wolves in the UP will depend more on how well humans and wolves get along than anything else. Unlike Wisconsin, the UP has a great deal of brushy habitat in large, publicly owned blocks. Biologists estimate the habitat could sustain anywhere from 400 to 800 wolves. That is what is referred to as the biological carrying capacity. Wolf numbers are more likely to be limited by the more elusive figure of the social carrying capacity – the number of wolves that people will tolerate. If wolves destroy pets and livestock, people will seek to reduce their numbers by legal or illegal means.

Michigan set its own standard for removing wolves from the state endangered species list. Wolves could be delisted, they decided, if the annual count didn't drop below 200 wolves for five successive years. That criterion has now been met. The wolf population continues to expand, although at a slower rate. It grew by 30 percent in some years. Recent years have seen growth of about 15 percent, suggesting Michigan's wolves are beginning to fill the best habitat available to them in the UP.

In 2003, federal authorities reduced the status of Michigan wolves from endangered to threatened. That allowed Michigan to create a depredation control program. Managers are eager to minimize conflicts between wolves and humans, so they are making a special effort to respond promptly to reports of depredation. In the first two years of the program, only seven wolves were destroyed.

Michigan's DNR managers are currently reworking an old restoration plan that is now outdated. The old population goal was only 100 wolves. The new plan will aim for a steady population three or four times that size. And the new management plan will include provisions for managing wolves in the Lower Peninsula.

No wolves have been confirmed present in the Lower Peninsula since 1910. There have been many possible wolf sightings, however, and everyone knows it is just a matter of time before wolves cross over on winter ice to the unoccupied habitat of the Lower Peninsula. Management issues there will be far more complicated than in the UP, although not essentially different from those being faced already in Minnesota and Wisconsin.

Isle Royale

Isle Royale is a beautiful, 45-mile long island in Lake Superior lying 20 miles (32 km) off the Minnesota shore. The island is managed as a wilderness-style national park, the most remote park in the US system. Moose swam to the island around 1900. With no predators to control their numbers, moose experienced an erratic boom-bust cycle for decades. In the winter of 1949, an ice bridge to the mainland allowed a wolf pack to migrate to the island and begin exploiting its bounty of moose.

Researchers long ago realized Isle Royale offered a unique setting for studying predator-prey relationships because there is so little impact on the ecosystem by humans. In 1958, Durward Allen began a scientific study of the Island's moose-wolf relationship. In this study, the researchers merely observe. Nothing is done to alter the balance between moose and wolves, and now this is the most thoroughly studied predator-prey relationship in the world.

An issue of concern has been the narrow genetic base of both wolves and moose. Today's populations of each species derive from a single pair. When wolf numbers dropped dangerously low a few years ago, some researchers assumed inbreeding might be a factor. Then wolf numbers went up again.

Wolf and moose numbers had soared and dipped in complex patterns over the decades. The moose population has ranged from 500 to 2,500. Wolf numbers have been as low as 11 and as high as 50. And as time has gone on, researchers have understood that the relationship is far more complicated than a simple two-species predator-prey relationship.

People usually assume that predators control how numerous the prey will be. But it is equal-

Wolf restoration in Wisconsin was hit hard by an outbreak of parvovirus, which killed a great many pups.

ly true that the abundance of the prey dictates how many predators can be alive at any time. In turn, the size and health of moose populations is directly impacted by the quality of their browse. The quality of the browse depends on how heavily it has been munched by moose as well as by discrete weather events and fluctuations in climate. Populations of both moose and wolves, in other words, are locked in a complex relationship that also includes many habitat and climate variables.

Currently, the island is home to 29 wolves in three packs (not counting pups). Moose numbers stand at 750, down from 1,100 just two years ago. Moose are doing badly these days, which will help wolves in the short run. Researchers think that warmer weather – possibly related to global warming – has stressed moose. Moose are unable to feed actively in hot weather, and when they weaken, wolves find them easy prey. Of course, if wolves bring the moose population down low, wolves will eventually pay a price for that. And so it goes.

The northeastern US

The conflict over prospects for restoring wolves to the northeastern US highlights a central dispute about the true nature of the Endangered Species Act (ESA). Wolf restoration has been markedly successful in the states of the western Great Lakes, and nobody can argue that gray wolves are in any danger of becoming extinct in North America. Yet many wolf fans want to go far beyond that, restoring wolves in as much suitable habitat as possible. In particular, some wolf advocates are enthusiastic about bringing wolves back in the northeastern part of the US.

Federal managers argue that the ESA places no burden on them to restore wolves "everywhere" or even in a major percentage of former wolf range. They read the act as tasking them with protecting wolves against extinction, which they have done. These managers aren't out to save the natural world, in other words; they see their responsibility as making sure that some specific species – the gray wolf in this case – remain viable.

Many environmentalists take a broader view. In their eyes, the ESA is a law with unique powers for redressing old wrongs and rehabilitating blighted ecosystems. These people argue that wolves belong in all portions of their former range where there is enough brushy habitat and food to sustain them. As the keystone predator of large ungulates, wolves play a critical role in an ecosystem, a role with consequences that reverberate throughout the system. These people point out that gray wolves have only been restored to something like three percent of their original range in the US.

Wolf fans and advocacy groups have long dreamed of restoring wolves to areas of the Northeast where the howl of a wolf has not been heard in about a century. A 1992 USFWS modification of the recovery plan for gray wolves identified a number of areas where wolf restoration might be possible. Included were Adirondack Park and areas of Maine and New Hampshire. In 2000, Bruce Babbitt, then the secretary of the interior, announced that wolf restoration in the Northeast "is significant and will contribute to the overall restoration of the species." No such statements have been made recently. It might seem odd that wolves would be a partisan issue, and yet Republicans have been historically less enthusiastic about wolves than Democrats. It is no coincidence that wolves were restored to Yellowstone Park during a Democratic administration.

Should wolves be restored to the Northeast? It isn't a simple issue.

In favor of wolf restoration is the fact there is abundant habitat and a strong prey base (moose, deer, and beaver). Adirondack Park, with six million acres (24,281 km^2), is the largest park in the US. Studies have concluded that there is enough habitat and prey to support at least a few wolf packs there.

Attitudes toward wolves are improving in the Northeast, as shown by surveys of public attitudes. Unlike the western US, there is not a powerfully entrenched livestock industry to oppose wolves in the Northeast, although there are farms with sheep, cattle, and horses. Wolf proponents argue that the ecosystem would benefit from the presence of the original keystone predator: the wolf. Even though the coyotes of New England are exceptionally robust, they are not wolves and cannot fill the same ecological niche.

And yet there are problems. The region's wolf habitat is highly fragmented. The Northeast lacks the large national parks and national forests that have been the cradle of wolf restoration in the western Great Lakes states. In Adirondack Park, for example, private and public lands are intermixed like a patchwork quilt. It is a land ownership pattern that seems doomed to maximize wolf-human conflicts. Maine and New Hampshire have passed bills announcing their opposition to wolf restoration.

A new complication is uncertainty about which wolf should be restored to the Northeast. Was the region's original wolf the red wolf or the wolf of Algonquin Park (if that is a different animal)? Or was it another wolf? Or was it a gray wolf? Taxonomists are not sure. If it is the red wolf or the Algonquin wolf, will that animal succumb to genetic swamping in the Northeast, where coyote populations are high? At least one researcher believes the wolf living in the Laurentide region of Quebec might be the original wolf of New England. That wolf seems a good candidate for the Northeast. It is large enough to take down moose and does not hybridize with coyotes.

There is some chance wolves will restore themselves in this region, as they did in Michigan, by coming into the area across winter ice. Large numbers of wolves live north of Maine, in Quebec. They are isolated from the US by the St. Lawrence Seaway, which is kept open by icebreakers in winter. Ice bridges still do form from time to time, and there have been many sightings (some confirmed) of wolves that apparently crossed over from Quebec. Any wolves that manage to slip across the border will face long odds for survival, as they'll not have the protection of endangered-species status.

The recent decision by USFWS to declare wolves restored to viability in the Eastern DPS means that the agency isn't going to make a priority of restoring wolves to the Northeast. This is sure to trigger a lawsuit by several environmental groups committed to seeing wolves return to the Northeast.

Delisting

In July of 2004, the USFWS held a press conference to announce that the gray wolf in the Eastern DPS is ready to come off the endangered species list. This DPS area consists of the northeastern quarter of the US and includes the states of Minnesota, Wisconsin, and Michigan, the states for which the original 1978 wolf-recovery plan had been written (see page 33). At the time of the announcement, over 3,000 wolves lived in the three states. Delisting would return wolf management responsibility to the respective states and some Native American tribes.

It was a festive occasion. The announcement was made under a bright white party tent erected on the grounds of the Wildlife Science Center, near Forest Lake, Minnesota. People took turns giving speeches about this remarkable achievement. The keynote address was given by Walter Medwid, the director of the International Wolf Center. He had to wait for several minutes when his speech was drowned out by a grand group howl from the 53 resident wolves. In this contest between wolves and man, wolves won.

Everyone sitting under the tent that sparkling morning understood, however, that the decision being celebrated is highly controversial. Given the nature of wolf politics, it would be astonishing if it had not been. Critics will challenge the delisting decision with multiple lawsuits. Most or all of the critics will be wolf advocate groups. The wolf won't actually come off the list until several issues have been tested in court, a process that will take years.

While delisting opponents will raise a number of objections, their arguments will mainly fall into two categories. One major argument will be that delisting now violates the ESA because it is premature. And it is premature, they argue, because the ESA actually requires the USFWS to introduce wolves to the Northeast.

Other critics will protest specific provisions of the programs the states have drafted to manage wolves, arguing that they seriously threaten the future of wolves. The delisting process requires states to submit acceptable management programs showing they can be responsible stewards of restored wolf popula-

Walter Medwid, director of the IWC, gives the keynote address at the USFWS delisting ceremony.

tions. The USFWS has approved plans from all states, although Michigan's plan is so out of date it is being totally revised.

The adequacy of these plans will be contested in the courts. Environmental groups will argue that they do not offer sufficient protection for wolves. Federal and state managers wrote their plans knowing they would have to defend them in court, and they are confident they will withstand this critical review.

Minnesota struggled to produce a plan that would be acceptable to the state legislature and yet satisfy federal managers. The plan creates two zones. Management in Zone A, which essentially includes the northeastern quarter of the state, would offer wolves a high degree of protection. Management in Zone B, the rest of the state, would be less wolf-friendly, with a less vigorous level of protection for wolves. The plan includes procedures for removing depredating wolves and arrangements to monitor the state's wolf population. Under the plan, there will be no public taking (shooting or trapping) of wolves for at least five years.

Wisconsin's plan is essentially similar. It has two core wolf zones, one enclosing the prime wolf range of the northern counties and another encompassing the central hardwoods zone around the Black River State Forest. Wolves in Zones 1 and 2 would receive a high level of protection. At the present time, 88 packs live in Zone 1 and 15 live in Zone 2. Zone 3 is defined as a buffer area that includes important dispersing travel lanes. Control measures on depredating wolves in this area would be fairly aggressive. Zone 4 is the highly settled portion of the state, where there really is no appropriate wolf habitat and where control on troublesome wolves would be severe.

Both plans include robust wolf control and depredation compensation programs. To some wolf advocates, this looks like a return to the "bad old days" of killing wolves. Some wolf advocates simply do not trust states to manage wolves appropriately. Some veteran wolf researchers worry more about a public backlash against wolves if these measures are not put in place to minimize wolf-human conflict. Without effective protection and compensation programs, they say, the gains wolves have made in public acceptance could be lost.

Toward the future

It turns out the math was simpler than we thought. We used to believe that *tolerance + deer + wilderness = wolves*. But no, it turns out that *tolerance + deer = wolves*. If you've got enough deer and tolerance, you don't need wilderness to produce strong numbers of wolves. As people have come to accept wolves, wolves have thrived.

It is too early to claim victory. Some wolf managers in the western Great Lakes states feel the "honeymoon" period of wolf restoration is about over. Wolf populations soared as wolves saturated empty habitat. Wolves have benefited from modern record numbers of deer, which have helped wolves keep out of trouble. As wolf populations build, managers expect increasing friction with humans along the "colonization front," that region of semi-settled land where inexperienced dispersing wolves will encounter sheep, cattle, and people's pets.

The story is most impressive in Minnesota. Simply put, at no time in modern history have so many humans and so many wolves gotten along so well. Before this, nobody could point to any example of wolves and humans coexisting amicably. Nobody could argue that it was possible for wolves and humans to live closely in relative harmony. Now we know: *it is possible*. We didn't know that several years ago.

In winter of 2004, Minnesota Public Radio ran a call-in show on the topic of wolves. The guest expert was Dave Mech, widely regarded as the world's foremost wolf researcher. I listened with fascination, wondering how many calls would come from people who love wolves and how many would come from wolf haters. The first callers were all people who were enthusiastic about wolves.

A deer hunter called from his truck in the northern part of the state. Were wolves responsible for the fact he was seeing fewer deer from his stand? Mech assured him wolves weren't suppressing the deer population. Remarkably, the hunter seemed satisfied. He'd just been wondering.

Another deer hunter called to describe a recent encounter with a wolf. He had shot a buck with a bow. Before he could recover the deer, a wolf came along and claimed it for himself.

"This is it," I thought. "This is the guy who is going to start ranting about how wolves are ruining everything."

But the hunter was just telling a story. He was emphatic about not feeling threatened by the wolf.

"I was thinking," he said, "*how many people ever get to see something like this?*"

By the end of the hour, *every* person calling into the show declared they were thrilled that Minnesota is home to so many wolves.

We've come a long way. Okay, it was *public* radio. Still, we've come a long way.

Never in history have wolves and people coexisted as well as they have recently in the western Great Lakes region.

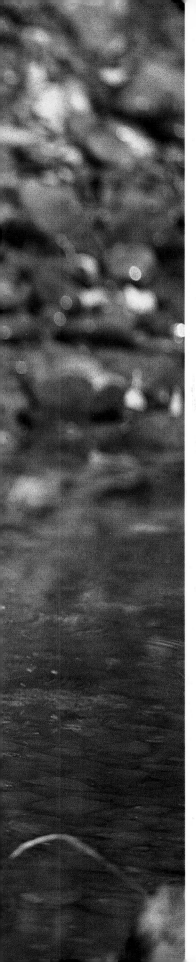

CHAPTER 10

Wolves of the West

When they found his body, the old wolf was lying curled up in a stand of aspen beside his last kill, a forkhorn elk. Wolf B2 looked so peaceful that the men almost expected him to rise and lope off. But he hadn't moved in several days and would not do so again.

He was called Wolf B2 by managers, who discourage personalizing the animals they handle. But even managers found it difficult to regard B2 unemotionally. He was special. Many began calling him The Old Man. To the Nez Perce, he was Chat Chaat (Older Brother).

B2 began life in the Hay River Valley, 30 miles east of Jasper National Park, in Alberta. He was born in 1990 or 1991. And he came extremely close to dying as a young wolf. The country around Jasper bristles with traps and snares, and B2 was caught in a snare. The trapper intended to sell his pelt for $150, in which case B2 would probably have become the trim for a luxurious coat.

Improbably, B2's life was spared because the US government had just offered to pay Canadian trappers $2,000 apiece for healthy wolves from packs that knew how to hunt elk. Managers needed live wolves to recolonize Yellowstone Park and central Idaho. B2 became one of those émigrés instead of a coat.

In January of 1995, B2 was placed in a kennel and flown to Montana with 11 other wolves. After a last-ditch legal maneuver to stop the release failed, B2 made another short flight to Missoula. The plane was met by representatives of the Nez Perce Tribe. The tribe had volunteered to be partners with US Fish and Wildlife Service (USFWS) managers in the effort to restore wolves to the Rockies.

Horace Axtell is a Nez Perce tribal elder who wants to revitalize his community by restoring a connection to its spiritual past. The tribe hoped that wolf restoration would reunite tribal members, individually and as a group, with their traditional religion. Axtell was just a boy when wolves disappeared from the Rockies, breaking the holy circle of life.

Axtell's meeting with the wolves was emotional. After singing a song to welcome the wolves, Axtell knelt to look into one of the kennels, his long gray braids brushing the ground. B2 turned his head and studied Axtell with calm interest. Axtell said softly, "Welcome back, brother."

B2 and three other wolves were hauled by truck deep into the Frank

Church Wilderness. After a harrowing four-hour ride on icy roads, the crates were placed on the ground the doors opened. The second wolf to bolt out was B2. He wore a radio collar painted red and black by Nez Perce school children who had taken an interest in the project.

B2 dashed out of his cage, stopped to pee, and then disappeared into the brush of the Frank Church Wilderness. There he remained for months, invisible except when located by researchers who homed in on his collar. On one of those occasions they were delighted to see B2 drive a mountain lion off an elk kill.

This was the time when B2 began acquiring his mystique as an elusive, lone wolf. He traveled widely, apparently without the company of other wolves. Researchers rarely could locate his radio signal.

Then, late in 1996, B2 disappeared completely. Researchers wondered if his collar had failed. They knew he might be a dead, yet occasional rumors surfaced in 1997 of a wolf with a red and black collar in north-central Idaho. For over a year, B2 was more of a rumor than a real wolf.

In 1998, it seemed B2 was everywhere. He appeared well south of his former wilderness haunts along the East Fork of the Salmon River. He moved around Ketchum and Sun Valley, slinking through the back yards of Idaho's wealthy wilderness lovers without being detected. And he had company. Although he'd been a lifelong bachelor, the seven- or eight-year old wolf had finally found a mate. She was B66, a former member of the Stanley Basin Pack. The pair settled into the Copper Basin area, a valley southeast of Sun Valley. The family they formed was named the Wildhorse Pack. B2 and B66 had pups in 2000 and 2001.

In the winter of 2001, B2's collar gave out and needed to be replaced. The man who tranquilized him with a sure shot from the helicopter was Carter Niemeyer, one of the most famous wolf managers in the world. Niemeyer holds a sensitive position as the USFWS's point man for dealing with depredating wolves in the northern Rockies. In that capacity, Niemeyer has killed or authorized the killing of hundreds of wolves. Niemeyer admires wolves, but he is committed to wolf control as a way of reducing friction between wolves and humans.

Niemeyer was impressed with the health of B2. The old wolf was by this time at least 10, extremely old for a wild wolf. B2's body was lean and muscular, although his cloudy eyes revealed that cataracts were stealing his eyesight. In the next year, B2 almost surely went totally blind, yet remained healthy. Researchers speculate that he was cared for by his pack. In the same circumstances, other wolf packs have killed or driven away pack members with serious impairments.

In the spring of 2001, rancher Dave Nelson began losing cattle. He told Niemeyer he suspected wolves. As president of the Idaho Cattle Association, Nelson was a powerful, well-connected man. He and Niemeyer had a tense discussion.

"I told him we'll kill the wolves around him," Niemeyer later said, "but we wouldn't kill B2."

"Everybody wanted to coddle that old boy," Nelson mused, "and I said I could accept that."

Government trapper Rick Williamson swooped up Fox Creek in a helicopter, passing the den site. The wolves had just killed another of Nelson's calves. B2, in fact, ran off still gripping one leg of the calf. Niemeyer was on the radio right away to tell Williamson he didn't want B2 shot. Trappers eventually caught one of the young females from the pack. When she was moved to Montana, the calf-killing stopped. B2's life had been spared a second time.

That winter, the winter of 2001, B2 and B66 moved south to new territory just north of the Craters of the Moon National Monument. Williamson happened to be in the area when he heard B66's collar beeping in mortality mode, meaning the wolf had not moved in several hours. B66's injuries showed she had been killed in an encounter with an elk.

Wolf restoration has gone better in the northern Rockies than many expected.

B2 suddenly began roaming wildly. Researchers speculated he might have been searching for B66. By the end of 2002, B2 was back along the East Fork of the Salmon River. He showed up in the corrals of a rancher but passed through, ignoring the livestock.

In 2003, B2 had another surprise for researchers. The old wolf had found another mate and sired another litter. This became known as the Castle Peak Pack. Curt Mack, the biologist leading the Nez Perce wolf program, spotted the old wolf on several flights over the Sawtooth National Recreation Area. Mack didn't fly too close to "The Old Man," as he didn't want to stress the aging wolf.

Late in the winter of 2004, B2's collar went into mortality mode. A few days later, Curt Mack and a graduate student hiked up Herd Creek, homing in on the signal from B2's collar. The old wolf lay curled up by his last elk. He could have suffered the fate of his first mate, dying of a kick from the elk. But it seems unlikely that a blind wolf would have engaged in a fight with prey. More likely, the old wolf was just too tired to move when his pack left the kill. He might have lain down by a food supply and simply died there. If so, his death was as unusual as his life, for wolves typically die of starvation or "with their boots on" in some kind of violent encounter. B2 was at least 14 when he died, making him possibly the oldest wild wolf on record.

When a young B2 sprinted out of his crate into the wilderness in 1995, he was the second wolf known to be in Idaho. The population was somewhere close to 375 when he died.

There is talk of erecting a statue to the wolf known as B2, Chat Chaat, and The Old Man.

The great campaign

The effort to eradicate wolves from the western US was often called a "campaign," and it had many qualities of a military campaign that involved conventional, chemical, and biological warfare. In 1905, Montana cattlemen forced passage of a bill mandating veterinarians to infect wolves with mange and release them to infect others.

Much of the killing was done with strychnine. Millions of wolves and coyotes died, plus untold numbers of badgers, foxes, hawks, eagles, and other unintended victims. Cattlemen poisoned horses, cattle, dogs, and even some of their own children.

Such carnage is easy to repudiate today, but it is hard to catch a sense of the times from which it arose. Market hunting radically reduced wild ungulate populations by the end of the 19th century. With no chance to make an honest living, wolves turned to livestock, and there is no questioning the fact they caused serious losses on some ranches.

As a result of the work of government predator control agents and private individuals, the work of wolf eradication went briskly. Viable wolf populations had mostly disappeared from most western states by the 1920s. The last

The wolf war had mostly eliminated wolves from the West by the 1920s.

wolf in Wyoming was killed on the Wind River Indian Reservation in 1943. Information is less clear about Idaho, but by the 1930s wolf sightings were rare.

Because park managers distinguished between "good" and "bad" animals, wolves weren't even safe in parks. Between 1914 and 1926, at least 136 wolves were killed in Yellowstone. The last two wolf pups in Yellowstone were destroyed in 1924.

The restoration debate

Appropriately, the first voice speaking for returning wolves to Yellowstone Park belonged to Aldo Leopold. Arguing in 1944 against the ignorance of measuring all animals in terms of their economic worth, Leopold explained that an ecological system is meant to function as a whole, with each species in the system playing an essential role.

After the Endangered Species Act (ESA) was adopted, the USFWS was tasked with preparing a plan to restore wolves in the northern Rockies. Early efforts were marked by bureaucratic timidity. And with good reason: The powerful livestock industry and many prominent politicians adamantly opposed wolf restoration. But the ESA is a strange and stubborn law. It put in motion some machinery that took on a life of its own.

The Yellowstone wolf debate turned into one of those great symbolic struggles that mark watershed moments in a society's history. At one level, the fight was about wolves, but at another level everyone understood that the Yellowstone wolf controversy was about who would get to define the future of the American West. For a century, livestock producers had enjoyed nearly perfect freedom to run things as they chose on their own lands. They hated the prospect of wolves attacking their livestock under legal protection that wouldn't allow them to defend their own stock.

Many other issues got sucked into the debate. Some westerners saw wolf restoration as an assault on state's rights and the freedom of westerners to manage their lives by traditional values. Ranchers naturally measure the worth of animals in economic terms, and in those terms wolves were worse than useless. To them, talk about ecological balance was utterly alien. Ranchers were threatened by the increasing popularity of a way of looking at animals that seemed to them odd and sentimental.

Environmentalists saw the fight as the ultimate test of the ESA. The absence of predators had resulted in a park that was wildly out of balance, with an elk herd that was obviously much too large. Elk were doing serious damage in the park and making themselves a nuisance on surrounding ranches when they left it, breaking fences and eating crops. If wolves could be barred from a place they so obviously belonged, environmentalists knew, the ESA would be reduced to a paper tiger. If the ESA meant anything at all, it meant wolves should be returned to Yellowstone. Contrarily, if the ESA could restore the world's most controversial predator to the American West, the act would be invigorated by that success.

The fur really flew when the USFWS issued a draft of a plan that proposed restoring wolves to the northern Rockies. According to the plan, wolves would be reintroduced to Yellowstone and a large block of wilderness in central Idaho. Montana Senator Conrad Burns predicted that if wolves were restored to the park, "There'll be a dead kid within a year." The American Farm Bureau dug in its heels and swore there would be "no wolves, nowhere, no how!"

Among advocates for wolves was John Varley, chief of research at Yellowstone. "If we restore wolves to Yellowstone," said Varley, "it will be the only place left in the 48 states that has all of the native animals and plants that were here when white men hit the shores of North America. Now there are none. Why can't we have just one place like that?"

Wolf advocates began educating the public about the realities of wolves. In 1983, the conservation group Defenders of Wildlife brought

wolves were coming back to the American West – like it or not – and that everyone would be better off if wolves came back under management protocols flexible enough to respond to depredations. "Let us have wolves," wolf advocates were saying, "and we promise to deal with those that misbehave." It was a sort of Faustian bargain that made many wolf fans uneasy – and continues to do so today when managers kill individual wolves or even whole packs of wolves that acquire the habit of attacking livestock.

The Nez Perce

As federal managers planned to move wolves to Yellowstone and central Idaho, they sought assistance from local managers. Politicians in Idaho refused to cooperate. The state legislature passed a bill forbidding state natural resource managers to aid wolf restoration.

That's when the Nez Perce tribe volunteered to be the local manager of wolf restoration.

The tribe offered to do wolf education projects for the general public but also to take on the hard work of tracking and keeping records on a group of elusive animals.

Needless to say, the US government had never before partnered with an Indian tribe to manage an endangered species, but USFWS leaders instantly saw the logic of the arrangement. Unlike federal managers, the Nez Perce were not outsiders. They knew the local people and the local ways of doing things. Moreover, in the words of wolf-recovery program coordinator Ed Bangs, "They bring a different attitude about wolves – a reverence for wildlife is part of their heritage."

The Nez Perce traditionally have respected wolves. The tribe identified with wolves, too, because both Indians and wolves suffered similar fates as European settlers assumed dominance in the West, dealing harshly with unruly Indians and unruly wolves. The Nez Perce religion includes the notion that all creatures on

Researcher Dave Mech is the man most directly responsible for wolf restoration. He knows his subject.

Earth form a circle of life. The wolf was missed as a vital part of that circle.

The tribe hired a competent wildlife biologist, Curt Mack, to run their program. The mix of modern science and traditional spirituality has worked better than anyone could have hoped.

Canadian wolves translocated to Yellowstone

In December of 1994, Canadian trappers began collecting wolves from an area of Alberta near Jasper National Park. Weeks later, helicopters flew low over brushy islands to flush wolves into the open, giving dart-gun marksmen chances to shoot them.

The wolves they collected were examined and fitted with radio collars. Biologists analyzed them for age, sex, and probable pack status. Then they shipped them to Yellowstone and Idaho.

To discourage them from leaving the park, the Yellowstone wolves would be given a "soft release." As had been done with red wolves in North Carolina, these wolves would be held for some time in pens so they would acquire a sense of belonging to the area of the park. Human contact was kept to a minimum. Wolves released in Idaho were given a "hard release."

On January 12, 1995, the first Canadian wolves were brought into Yellowstone Park in aluminum kennels. After last-ditch legal maneuvering played out, the wolves were moved to their various acclimation pens in sites around the park. Wolf advocates, some of whom had been in battle for ten years to see this happen, stood by and cheered. Late in March, 14 wolves were set free in Yellowstone Park. All in all, in 1995 and 1996, 33 Canadian wolves were released in Yellowstone.

The Idaho release attracted much less publicity. On January 14, four Canadian wolves were hard-released near Corn Creek. Soon

Wolf tracks and sign are easy to spot at Yellowstone nowadays.

A Yellowstone wolf observes wolf tourists as they observe a pack of wolves.

afterward, 11 more wolves were released near the Middle Fork of the Salmon River. Another 20 Canadian wolves were released in Idaho in 1996.

And they prospered. The wolves prospered even better than managers had expected. More translocations were originally planned, but the immediate success of wolves released in the first two years made that unnecessary. In 1996, four Yellowstone packs produced 14 pups. Idaho's wolves also got busy producing pups, and by the end of 1996 Idaho already had 41 wolves. By 1999, Yellowstone had 115 wolves, with at least 10 pairs raising litters. By 1999, Idaho had 120 wolves, including 10 to 13 breeding pairs.

Success

In a survey done in the summer of 2004,

USFWS managers documented the presence of 800 to 850 wolves in the northern Rockies, with 66 breeding pairs. Yellowstone Park itself has 12 breeding pairs and a total of about 169 wolves. Wolves are harder to observe in Idaho. Tribal and federal managers estimate about 29 packs and a total of about 368 wolves. In northwestern Montana, around Glacier Park, there are about 79 wolves. This Glacier Park wolf zone is smaller and less stable. It tends to cycle between a low of 50 to a high of 100 wolves.

Managers believed the 2004 population in the three recovery zones is about as high as it can get. Some speculate that there is not enough suitable habitat in the northern Rockies for more than 1,000 wolves, and even that figure might be high. Wolves have filled up the best living spaces for them, particularly in Yellowstone. Further population growth might send more and more dispersers out of the recovery zones, and those wolves will encounter a landscape that doesn't have many good places for wolves to live.

Managers claim they are pleased with the relatively low level of depredation problems in these zones. Wolves currently kill about 60 cattle each year, mostly calves, with sheep losses averaging about 200 a year. As a percentage of overall causes of losses, wolves rank low. That is, compared to weather, coyotes, disease, and accidents, wolves are responsible for a tiny percentage of livestock losses. From the perspective of livestock producers, however, wolf losses come on top of all other losses. From the perspective of politicians and anti-wolf activists, wolf depredation is a perfect symbolic issue for railing against the federal government.

Not all wolf fans are delighted with current management. In 2002, federal agents dealt harshly with the Whitehawk Pack in central Idaho after the pack repeatedly attacked livestock. They shot two pack members. When the pack preyed on sheep again days later, agents killed three more wolves. Days later, the pack killed a calf, and this time agents killed all remaining pack members.

The incident inflamed public opinion. Wolf opponents pointed to it as proof of how incorrigible wolves are. Wolf advocates were outraged at the slaughter of a whole pack. Some wolf fans winced and accepted this bloody event as the price that must be paid to have wolves in an American West that has so many livestock operations next to wild lands.

Wolf tourism

Wolves amazed researchers when they began conducting their daily affairs in full view of Yellowstone's visitors. The word soon got out that Yellowstone Park was the best place in the world to see wild wolves. Among the first wolf tourists were wolf managers who had worked a lifetime among wolves without actually see-ing them much.

Other visitors began arriving from all over the world. By 2004, over 130,000 visitors have observed wolves, with more wolf tourists showing up each year. Winter and early spring are more productive times to see wolves, but wolves are seen virtually every day. At one time it was unusual for anyone to see a wild wolf; at Yellowstone seeing wolves has become so common, at one time people spotted them daily for at least 1,100 days in a row.

Wolf watching is now the most popular activity in the park. The sport has become quite sophisticated. Now there are wolf-watching guides. Wolf watchers now come armed with powerful spotting scopes and two-way radios for signaling each other when a wolf makes an appearance.

Wolf tourism has had a significant economic impact. The figure most often quoted is that wolf tourism directly adds 20 million dollars to the economies of towns in the Yellowstone Park area. That figure needs to be considered in the context of all other costs of the program. However, Idaho has received little tourism from its even larger wolf population, as Idaho's wolves remain difficult to find and observe.

Why are Yellowstone's wolves so relaxed about being seen? While some observers have speculated that the wolves got accustomed to people while being held in the acclimation pens, managers scoff at that. Wolves are highly intelligent animals. Many of the wolves of Yellowstone have simply noticed that people pose no special threat to them and adjusted their behavior accordingly. Some of the wolves of Alaska's Denali Park have made the same adjustment.

Cascading impacts

Yellowstone Park has been hit with two cataclysmic changes in recent decades. A wildfire burned almost half of the park in 1988, and wolves returned in 1995. Both events have been highly controversial, with doomsayers predicting the death of the park in each case.

But just as fire seems to have rejuvenated the old park, wolves are affecting the park in ways that seem restorative.

While some researchers feel it is premature to talk about wolf impacts on the park, several early studies offer intriguing results. The biggest change seems to be in elk behavior. Elk used to mill around streams in herds like dairy cattle. The preferred browse of elk is the young shoots of willow, cottonwood, and aspen trees. As fast as those young trees emerged along Yellowstone's streams, elk grazed them off.

That has changed. Wolves can stalk elk more easily near the brush of streams. Elk have learned it is dangerous to loiter near streamside brush, so now they typically graze in open areas and spend more time moving about. The elk are now vigilant, having learned in recent years what wolves can do.

The impact on streamside vegetation has been dramatic. Thanks to wolves' influence on the elk, trees are growing along the streams just as they once did. The trees cast shade over the streams, favoring trout. Beaver have returned to the park's streams in big numbers since they now have young trees to eat along the banks. Beavers are building lodges and backing up streams with their dams, creating habitat for mink, muskrats, and ducks. Stream banks are now more stable, suffering less erosion, which improves the water quality.

The elk kills that wolves leave around the park are now consumed by ravens, magpies, golden eagles, bears, bald eagles, and coyotes. Coyote numbers have gone down by as much as 50 percent in some areas, which improves the survival prospects of some small mammals and birds. The loss of coyotes might have helped foxes, and so the small birds and mammals that fox feed upon are under new pressure. Biodiversity, overall, might be increasing.

This is a lot of change to explain by the presence of wolves, and there are skeptics. But scientists admit they are impressed by the cumulative cascading impacts of the return of the keystone predator to the park. Wolves are just one of the species present in the park, yet their return might have brought overall balance to the system. The circle of life has been restored.

Beyond the recovery zones

One of the most controversial topics related to wolf recovery is where wolves will show up next and whether they will establish self-sustaining populations outside the original three recovery zones.

Wolves are showing up in other western states. In 2002, a wolf was caught in a coyote trap in Utah. It had crossed the entire state of Wyoming. In the summer of 2004, a female wolf was fatally hit by a car along Interstate Highway 70, just west of Denver. That wolf had apparently moved 500 miles alone. In 1999, wolf B-45 wandered out of Idaho into Oregon. Similarly, wolf Y-206 walked out of Idaho and spent time in Washington before moving northwest into British Columbia. She was the first wolf confirmed in Washington since 1975.

Several states without wolves are now drafting plans for managing them if and when they show up. Oregon, Washington, and Colorado are forming plans. Oregon created a 14-member Wolf Advisory Committee with the task of creating a wolf plan. The plan, which is currently being subjected to public comment and criticism, anticipates that more wolves will come to Oregon until the state has a population. Wolves would be classified as "special status mammals" and managed to preserve at least four breeding pairs. If numbers exceed seven breeding pairs, hunting might be used to keep the population from expanding. Most observers feel the plan represents a reasonable compromise.

Of all states, Colorado has the most exciting potential for future wolf recovery. Wolves were extirpated there by the mid-1930s. In spite of rumors of sightings, only one wolf is confirmed to have been in the state since then. Biologists and wolf advocates argue that Col-

Wolf restoration faces new challenges as it tries to return wolves to the Southwest.

orado has a strong elk herd and a great deal of appropriate habitat. A 1994 study by Colorado College concluded that the state could sustain as many as 1,100 wolves. A poll taken at the same time found that 71 percent of Coloradoans supported wolf restoration.

Most authorities assume it is just a matter of time until wolves find their way to Colorado. The state is currently drafting a management plan to deal with wolves when they come. Plans are complicated by changes going on with federal efforts to delist the wolf in the northern Rockies.

When the USFWS recently revised its maps of Distinct Population Segments (DPS; see page 33), something exciting happened. A large block of states in the southwestern US has been classified "endangered," a designation that commits USFWS to restoring wolves to this region. The southern half of Colorado (south of Interstate Highway 70) falls in this Southwestern DPS.

Plans are being prepared that would accomplish that very challenging goal. One big unsettled issue is which wolf should be restored to the Southwest: the Mexican wolf, or the larger gray wolf now repopulating the Northern Rockies? A recovery team is wrestling with that and other key issues as this book goes to press. Whatever they propose will not happen

Visitors come from all over the world to view Yellowstone's wolves.

overnight. Political opposition is sure to be potent, and the whole process for planning and executing a recovery plan is slow and deliberate.

Not much can be said now about the future for wolf restoration in the American Southwest, including southern Colorado. It seems likely that this will be the last major USFWS effort to restore wolves in a general region of the country. And in spite of what is sure to be powerful resistance, USFWS seems committed to an ambitious effort to bring wolves back to a significant new region.

This will be the most interesting wolf restoration arena in the next decade or so.

Delisting

The original USFWS recovery plan for wolves in the Northern Rockies set a target of 10 breeding pairs in each of the three recovery areas, with that minimum level holding for three consecutive years. Then USFWS changed the recovery standard, in effect lumping wolves so that the goal became 30 breeding pairs overall rather than three groups of at least 10. One reason for this was the unsteady fortunes of the wolves in northwestern Montana. That population has tended to cycle rather than holding even or building steadily.

The redefinition of success was initially opposed by wolf groups because it seemed like "lowering the bar," accepting a lesser standard for wolf recovery. But when researchers documented that wolves move back and forth among the three recovery areas, the new minimum goal became less of an issue. There seems to be no danger that these three recovery areas will be isolated genetic islands, so it seems safe enough to work with the simpler goal of 30 breeding pairs.

Before USFWS can take the wolf off the endangered species list, the states involved with the wolf program must come up with management plans that meet USFWS approval. The key issue is whether, in the judgment of USFWS, each state has a plan that seems likely to manage wolves responsibly so they don't become endangered again. Montana and Idaho have plans for managing wolves that have been reviewed and approved by the USFWS. Some wolf fans hope Idaho improves its plan by incorporating the Nez Perce tribe in some significant way in the future.

The state of Wyoming, however, has taken a stand that threatens to tie up wolf delisting for many years. Ignoring hints that the management plan it was drafting would be unacceptable, Wyoming adopted a plan that offered wolves almost no protection. The plan would classify all wolves outside Yellowstone and Grand Teton parks as predators that could be hunted without any regulation, monitoring, or safeguards. Additionally, USFWS informed Wyoming that its plan failed to ensure the viability of wolves in two other regards.

Wolf fans feared that USFWS would accept Wyoming's plan, even with all of its flaws, because the service is eager to declare wolf restoration a success story and move on to other challenges. A panel of biologists and researchers did find the plan barely adequate from a scientific point of view. But USFWS didn't think the plan would stand up to judicial review when the inevitable lawsuits from pro-wolf groups tested it. Wyoming politicians, miffed because their plan was rejected, have brought a suit against the USFWS. Some

observers feel this battle could tie up delisting for as long as five years, during which time wolf management will remain in federal hands. This seems like a foolish waste of public tax money and a regrettably confrontational resolution to the dispute. By developing a reasonable program, Wyoming could have made it possible for three states to resume control over wolves.

Wyoming's tantrum presents wolf advocates with a mixed blessing. Wolves have thrived under USFWS management and will continue to do so. That is exactly what most wolf advocates have wanted. Senior researchers and managers, however, regret this lost opportunity to notch a dramatic victory for the ESA and for wolves. Wolves are not endangered and should be returned to state management in the northern Rockies. That's what the ESA is all about.

It has only been nine years since wolf B2 rocketed out of his kennel and disappeared into the wilderness of central Idaho. In those nine years, the population of wolves known to live in the northern Rockies has gone from zero to as many as 850. That is almost three times the minimum goal for delisting the wolf in the Northern Rockies. The biological challenges have been met with ease. But the political and social challenges look as daunting as ever.

Ed Bangs, the recovery coordinator for the USFWS's wolf-recovery program, recently pronounced himself pleased with the program on all counts. "I've been surprised at how little depredation there has been. The wolves have done better than we could have expected. The wolves have done great."

And how are humans doing?

"Oh, I don't know," said Bangs, sounding weary. "Those folks who love wolves before they got here . . . they still love 'em. Those folks who hated wolves before they got here . . . they still hate 'em."

CHAPTER 11

Hope for a Troubled Lobo Program

The first 11 Mexican wolves reintroduced to the American Southwest never had much of a chance. They had lived their whole lives in captivity. They didn't know how to find or kill prey. They knew nothing about the world they would inhabit – such things as where water could be found, what to do when encountering a cougar, or how risky it is to cross a highway where vehicles hurtle by at speeds incomprehensible to a wolf.

Nor did they have a clue about how dangerous some humans are. Some zoo-born wolves might have associated people with food. A biologist who used to work with some of these zoo-born animals once described them as "knucklehead wolves." Under the best of circumstances, some knucklehead wolves would have died in the wild.

They did not get the best of circumstances.

The 11 Mexican wolves were not just released into a dangerous world they didn't understand, they were inserted in the middle of a war between the Old West and the New West. The wolves were caught between ranchers and hunters on one side and environmentalists and recent migrants on the other. Just before the wolves were released, tensions were exacerbated by US Interior Department decisions that restricted grazing rights and cut back logging on public lands. From the perspective of many Southwesterners, the federal government was determined to destroy the economy and unique culture of the region they loved. While these folks couldn't shoot a federal bureaucrat, they sure could shoot a wolf.

It didn't help that the highly endangered Mexican wolves were liberated in land that is open to public hunting. Unlike Yellowstone or Glacier National Parks, the Blue Range Primitive Area of eastern Arizona and western New Mexico is a free-fire zone. The terrain is crosshatched with roads, and this is a region where pickups typically carry a loaded rifle in the back window. It is almost a reflex for folks to "pop a coyote" whenever they see one.

Less than a year after they were released, none of the original 11 translocated wolves remained in the wild. Necropsies on the bodies of five showed that they died from shots fired from five different rifles.

augmented when analyses showed that several wolves in zoos were true Mexican wolves. The genes of the "Aragón" and "Ghost Ranch" bloodlines added badly needed diversity to the program's foundation stock.

Rumors persist of wild lobos in remote regions of Mexico where travelers rarely go. These stories have never been confirmed, so managers must proceed with restoration using the animals in the program now.

Delay and recovery

In 1979, the USFWS created a Mexican Wolf Recovery Team. It produced a recovery plan signed by US and Mexican officials in 1982. The team had highly limited options. They would have to translocate animals born in captivity as had been done with the red wolf. Opposition to the program was ferocious, which meant the team needed all of the management flexibility of the "experimental and nonessential" clause of the ESA.

Mexico is supposed to create its own lobo restoration program. Little has happened so far because of budgetary limitations.

And not much happened in the US for years. The program wasn't funded adequately, plus there weren't enough Mexican wolves alive to allow managers to risk putting them out in a world bristling with rifles, highways, and livestock.

It didn't help that national wolf and environmental groups were so preoccupied with the titanic Yellowstone conflict that they mostly overlooked the lobo.

Critics grumbled that the USFWS had failed to make a priority of Mexican wolf restoration. But as a matter of political reality, the USFWS cannot arrogantly push forward with unpopular plans, even if a rigid law like the ESA seems to insist that it take action. Although little seemed to be happening, the advocacy and educational programs of various groups were preparing the groundwork.

In 1986, several wolf groups increased pressure on the USFWS, which asked three states

to cooperate by proposing suitable lands for wolf reintroduction. Texas stonewalled, claiming that there was not one spot in the state where wolves might be restored. Arizona was the most enthusiastic about wolves, and it proposed 15 potential recovery sites. New Mexico offered one: White Sands, a large facility used by the US Army as a practice range.

Naming White Sands as a potential wolf restoration site inflamed the opposition. Livestock and hunting interests organized to block wolf restoration. In 1987, an Army commander announced that White Sands would not accept wolves. A regional USFWS director stunned wolf fans by responding, "The wolf reintroduction program, as of now, is terminated."

Wolf advocates regrouped, forming the Mexican Wolf Coalition. It sued the US Department of Interior and Department of Defense. Prominent among the groups advocating for the Mexican wolf were Defenders of Wildlife, the Sierra Club, the Audubon Society, and P.A.WS. (Preserve Arizona's Wolves). This latter group, led tirelessly by wolf advocate Bobbie Holaday, raised thousands of dollars and conducted many public information programs.

The Army changed its mind about White Sands, but then USFWS changed *its* mind, concluding that there wasn't enough prey on White Sands to support wolves. But the logjam seemed to be broken. Congress appropriated a modest amount of money to fund Mexican wolf recovery.

The basic argument wolf advocates made to the livestock industry was that wolves *were* going to come back and only those who participated in the process would have any voice in how they would be managed. Stockmen finally realized that while adamant opposition was emotionally satisfying, it would marginalize them in wolf management debates. The Arizona Cattle Growers and the Arizona Wool

Wolf reintroduction can sometimes generate conflict with stockmen.

The lobo program has faced most of the challenges of the red wolf program, plus public hostility.

Producers adopted resolutions – reluctant, conditional resolutions – favoring wolf reintroduction.

It proved difficult to turn public support for wolves into actual wolf feet on the ground. A 1998 survey in New Mexico showed 79 percent of state residents wanted wolves restored. But ranchers are more vehement in their opposition than average citizens are about wanting wolves. The American political system is designed to make it difficult for a tepid majority to impose its will on a determined minority, especially a minority that is well connected to political leaders.

The restoration plan

In 1993 USFWS accepted a plan to begin releasing wolves. Managers thought the best habitat available to them was the Blue Range Primitive Area in eastern Arizona and south-western New Mexico.

The program would have modest goals. Mexican wolves could be considered restored, managers decided, when a population of at least 100 wolves successfully occupied an area 5,000 square miles (12,950 km^2) of the animal's historic range. They planned to meet this goal by 2005. Besides the wild lobos, managers wanted to keep a genetic base of 200 Mexican wolves living in approximately 30 breeding sites scattered widely around the country.

Almost everything was against the Mexican wolf program. It had every headache of the red wolf program, plus frenzied opposition like that faced in the northern Rockies wolf program, plus a few unique problems of its own. Like red wolf program managers, the lobo mangers had to work with captive-bred wolves. But while the red wolves released in the Alligator River area were protected by dense swamp, Mexican wolves would be released in country where people can see a long distance. North Carolinians had almost welcomed the red wolf with open arms, whereas the Mexican wolf program had shrill critics before it even got underway.

In the eyes of some lobo managers, the biggest single threat to the program was the heavy presence of cattle in the primary recovery zone. That almost guaranteed that wolves would come into conflict with people. This constant intermingling of cattle and wolves was a situation not faced by wolf restoration managers anywhere else. And because of the nasty political climate in the Southwest, managers felt compelled to accept some rules that threatened to cripple a program that already faced a daunting challenge.

Wolf halfway houses

Until a year or two ago, managers were mostly releasing captive-bred animals. The process of starting a release begins by selecting those animals from breeding facilities that seem like the most promising candidates for release. Captive-bred wolves qualify for release on the basis of genetic makeup and behavior.

To ease the transition from captivity to life in the wild, an extra step has been introduced in the form of pre-acclimation pens. These are sometimes called "wolf halfway houses." Wolves move from the breeding facilities to one of three pre-acclimation facilities where they are conditioned for life in the wild. The hope is that wolves will adjust to a diet of road-killed deer or elk and become a little wilder. Managers minimize contact with the wolves in these pre-acclimation pens and actually try to make any contacts the wolves have with people unpleasant. Managers don't want wolves thinking people are their friends.

Wolves move from these halfway houses to acclimation pens close to the habitat that managers hope they'll adopt as their own. This is the usual "soft release" protocol but with the added step of the pre-acclimation pens.

The blue range

The Blue Range Wolf Recovery Area consists of the Apache National Forest and the adjacent Gila National Forest. The combined forests sprawl over the border between Arizona and New Mexico, with more land and better habitat on the New Mexico side. The size of the whole area is 4.4 million acres (17,700 km^2). The vegetation includes grass, pinyon, juniper, and oaks in lower regions, with mixed conifers at higher elevations.

While it is rugged, the area is open to public use and has a number of roads in it. Stockmen hold permits to run as many as 82,000 head of cattle on the area. Both white-tailed and mule deer are common, and elk numbers are high.

There is poetry in choosing the Blue Range for the lobo release site. It was here that Aldo Leopold worked as a young forester. Leopold's moving description of killing a wolf in the essay "Thinking Like a Mountain" (see page 23) helped change public perceptions of wolves. That shooting took place in the Blue Range.

Difficult beginnings

As we have seen, because there was so much opposition to wolves in New Mexico, managers accepted some crippling compromises on management protocol. The better wolf habitat lies on the New Mexico side, but managers agreed they would stock wolves only on the Arizona side. Even odder was the agreement that wolves could be released in New Mexico only after they had been released in Arizona and then recaptured for some reason. So if a wolf was released in Arizona and later recaptured because it attacked a cow, it could then be re-released in New Mexico.

Another regrettable compromise requires program staffers to capture and remove any wolves that occupy range out of the recovery zone. This rule applies to any wolf, not just those that bother cattle. No such provision exists in any other wolf restoration program.

The release of those first 11 wolves in 1998 seemed to mark the successful end of a long, difficult road to actually get wolves on the ground. The Campbell Blue pack was an adult pair and two yearlings. The Hawk's Nest pack was an adult pair and two two-year-old offspring. The Turkey Creek group was a pair.

All in all, the knuckleheads didn't do that badly. They learned to hunt and kill elk. Although surrounded by cattle herds, they avoided cattle. One pair produced a pup, the first wild-born wolf in the Southwest in over two decades. That pup was born to the Campbell Blue pair. When the female was shot, the male tried to raise the pup. Then the pup went missing and researchers assume it died. At that point, the male became flaky and began hanging around people and cattle, although he seemed harmless. He was eventually recaptured so he could be given a fresh chance at life in the wild.

Others didn't do that well. Wolf 494 took to digging trash near a restaurant outside Alpine, Arizona. That terrified some townsfolk, although the only aggression this wolf committed was an attack on a chicken coop that netted her three chicks and a duck. She later suffered the ignominy of getting beaten up by a mule while a crowd of stunned tourists stood by watching. She was recaptured.

Soon there were no wolves left in the wild.

Dead wolves

The first documented shooting incident triggered a controversy about law enforcement. A man named Richard Humphries was camping with his family and his dog at an unauthorized site near the territory of the Turkey Creek pair. These wolves had shown a tendency to associate with dogs. Humphrey shot the male wolf, claiming he felt it had threatened his family. Later he changed stories, but forensic evidence didn't back either story. USFWS officials decided against prosecuting because they didn't want to make a martyr of a man who might be seen in his region as a hero, defending his family against a wolf. Wolf advocates were heartsick.

Then four more wolves were shot in subsequent weeks. Some wolf fans decided there had to be a conspiracy behind so many wolf killings. There were rumors of a "bounty" on wolves backed by stockmen, but nothing was proved. Militant wolf advocates blamed USFWS for not prosecuting the first case. Other wolf advocates felt the whole situation was so tense that prosecuting Humphries would have exacerbated an already volatile environment.

It was no surprise that the first wolves released had trouble, although more wolves were shot than anyone could have predicted. An ugly truth about this kind of program is that many of the first generation of captive-bred wolves will die or misbehave. Managers have to put out more and more animals in spite of painful losses and setbacks. In time, some captive-bred animals will successfully raise a litter of wild-born pups. And then, in a year or two, those wild-born pups will bring off a litter of their own. That is when the program really begins to work.

Political ups and downs

Built in to the USFWS recovery plan is a requirement for three- and five-year reviews. The three-year review was conducted by a distinguished panel of researchers headed by Canada's Paul Paquet. In June of 2001, the panel released an 80-page report. Their sobering conclusion: The program was on the right track but probably wouldn't achieve its goals without significant improvements.

The panel recommended that USFWS alter two stupid rules that were hobbling its effectiveness. First, the panel wanted managers to be free to release wolves directly to Arizona's portion of the recovery area. The review panel also criticized the arrangement obliging lobo managers to remove any wolves living outside the recovery zone. This arrangement hurt the program by forcing staff to waste time chasing after wolves that had done nothing wrong.

Finally, the panel asked USFWS to insist that

ranchers running cattle on public land remove the carcasses of dead cows. Many of the lobos that got in trouble with cattle acquired a taste for beef by scavenging corpses left to rot on public land.

From the start, the Mexican wolf recovery program has involved an unusual coalition of many different governmental agencies. The major cooperating agencies are USFWS, Arizona Department of Game and Fish, New Mexico Department of Game and Fish, US Department of Agriculture Wildlife Services, US Department of Agriculture Forest Services, and the White Mountain Apache Tribe.

Some of these groups became unhappy with poor communications and coordination. That led to a significant restructuring of the program in 2002 along the lines of "adoptive man-agement," which is an organizational model that encourages adaptations based on experience.

This coalition was strengthened in May of 2004 when the New Mexico Game Commission finally endorsed wolf restoration. New Mexico has been a partner from the start, although sometimes a conflicted partner. The New Mexico Game Commission advises and influences natural resource management. After Governor Bill Richardson placed a number of fresh faces on the commission, the group reversed its long record of opposition to wolves. "It's safe to say, historically, that New Mexico has been a less-than-enthusiastic partner in wolf reintroduction. I hope by signing this agreement that we change that perception," said one commissioner.

Many consider the handsome lobo the most unique and endangered subtype of gray wolf in North America.

Indians for and against wolves

The White Mountain Apache Tribe announced in 2004 that it had made the first release of Mexican wolves on tribal lands. The tribe liberated a breeding pair and their pups in the southeastern portion of the reservation. The White Mountain Apaches have long supported wolf restoration for the same cultural and spiritual reasons as the Nez Perce in Idaho. In 2000, the tribe hired its own wolf biologist. Ultimately, the tribe hopes to establish six packs on its reservation.

Despite their cultural traditions that support wolf restoration, Indians can be as diverse in attitudes toward wolves as whites. The San Carlos Apache Tribe has opposed wolves from the start. Their position, as summed up by a wolf manager, is: "You guys came here, subjugated the Apaches and put us on the reservation. Then you carved up and gave away parts of the reservation, leaving us with little. Then you told us, 'Here are some cattle. You should join the modern world by raising cattle.' Now you want to give us wolves to eat those cattle. No thanks. You can keep your wolves."

Tragedy and triumph

Mexican wolf numbers have climbed somewhat more slowly and less steadily than program planners had hoped. But the numbers have gone up. In 2002, wolves born in the wild gave birth to pups, a real milestone.

Lobos had a terrible year in 2003. Thirteen wolves died, at least six by gunshot. Managers were concerned because more than half the dead wolves were alphas. They wondered whether wolf reproduction would suffer because only the alpha pair of a pack will breed. To their delight, almost all packs had pups. The fact that so many packs bounced back from the loss of an alpha means that wolves are moving freely in their new territory and their social mechanisms are working well.

Program managers plan special efforts to reduce the number of wolves being shot. Wolf mortality by gunshot continues to be higher in the lobo program than anywhere else. The shootings are worst during hunting season, probably because more people are in the backcountry with rifles then.

In spite of continued shooting mortality, wolf numbers are going up. The total count late in 2004 was 50 to 60 wolves in the wild, including pups. In addition, approximately 250 Mexican wolves in captivity in over 40 zoos or other breeding facilities provide a protected pool of wolves, in case they are needed.

There are some heartening success stories. Wolf 511 was a pup with the Campbell Blue pack in the original 1998 release. When this pack wandered out of the recovery zone, they were trapped and reeled back in. Wolf 511 was paired up with a male and re-released. Since then, she has been one of the program's most successful breeders, with litters four years in a row. Wolf 511 has been relocated to prime habitat in the Gila National Forest, where she thrives. She must be a grandmother or great-grandmother by now, a wolf born in captivity but producing wild wolves.

Of the 50 to 60 wild wolves now running free, half had been born in the wild and have only known life in the wild. They are *wolves* in every sense. There are eight breeding pairs (another way of saying eight packs), with several unattached wolves moving around. At about 50 wolves, other wolf restoration programs took off. Lobo managers hope the same holds true in the Southwest.

Reflecting on the strident opposition Mexican wolves still face, a lobo manager recently said, "I think the biggest difference is that in the northern Rockies, the legal fights are all over. Managers have a good track record of working with ranchers when wolves take livestock. They've moved or shot a lot of wolves, proving good faith. Here, people still think they can stop the program. We're not yet at the point where people have accepted that wolves are here to stay. We're not yet at the point where enough people are ready to sit down with us and work together."

Southwest DPS

The Mexican wolf program faces big changes when the USFWS launches an ambitious campaign to restore wolves in a significant portion of the Southwest. The Southwest DPS is a major region wrapped around the much smaller Mexican wolf recovery area, the Blue Range. The plan to restore wolves in the Southwest is historically significant, for the Southwestern DPS will be only the third place where the USFWS has made a major effort to restore wolves in a region (the others being the Eastern DPS and the Western DPS; see the map on page 33).

Currently the USFWS is crafting a recovery plan for wolves in the Southwest DPS. At this writing nobody knows what that plan will look like. It might or might not involve releasing more Mexican wolves. It might or might not declare that restoring wolves in the Blue Range is sufficient to satisfy the requirements of the Endangered Species Act in the entire Southwest, in which case no more translocations will be attempted. The planning team has not yet decided what specific numerical population goals should be set.

Nor has the team decided which specific areas might get wolves, if managers decide to stock wolves outside the Blue Range Recovery Area. Speculation points to several promising areas with good habitat and enough prey to sustain wolves. One is the southern Rockies (including Rocky Mountain National Park, Gunnison National Recreation Area, and southern Colorado's San Juan Mountains). Another promising area is the Grand Canyon and the adjacent Kaibab Plateau. At this time, nobody can say if wolves will be translocated anywhere in the Southwest in the future, but a good guess would be that they will and that these are the areas where they'll be put.

All that lies in the future. It is painful to contemplate all the contentious discussions lying ahead for those plans. Meanwhile, there seems to be new vitality in a program that has faced brutal challenges and suffered its share of setbacks.

"As usual," says program coordinator Colleen Buchanan, "the wolves have come through in great fashion. The wolves have performed beautifully. It's the people that are so hard to manage."

And now the howl of wolves is heard again rolling down the canyons of the Blue Range. Aldo Leopold described it once:

> A deep chesty bawl echoes from rimrock to rimrock, rolls down the mountain, and fades in to the far blackness of the night. It is an outburst of wild defiant sorrow, and of contempt for all the adversities of the world.

At the time he wrote, wolves were gone from the Gila River wilderness, and Leopold had no hope they would return. He would smile to know they are back.

CHAPTER 12

Alaska's Wolf Wars

In 1939, a lean young biologist named Adolph Murie hiked into Alaska's Mount McKinley (now Denali) Park to begin a series of field studies that would change wolf management forever. Murie was hired by the US National Park Service to help the agency manage the few wolves still living in its parks. Throughout the early decades of the 20th century, the service eradicated cougars, wolves, and coyotes from national parks. Everybody knew predators didn't belong in parks. They killed other animals.

In the 1930s, some progressive voices challenged park managers to reconsider the legitimacy of predators. Some naturalists suggested that parks could become sanctuaries for predators. The park service wanted solid information confirming or denying whether wolves were decimating the Dall sheep of Mount McKinley National Park.

Murie's equipment was simple. The most sophisticated gear he packed in was a pair of binoculars. Nothing Murie brought with him was worth as much as his keen interest and integrity. As he observed the daily lives of the East Fork pack of wolves, Murie carefully filled dozens of field notebooks. He later turned those notebooks into his book, *The Wolves of Mount McKinley*.

Today, Murie is best remembered today for his observation that wolves are not vicious. He noted, "The strongest impression remaining with me after watching the wolves on numerous occasions was their friendliness. The adults were friendly toward each other and amiable toward the pups . . . ."

That radically nonjudgmental view of wolves marked the beginning of the new appreciation for them.

Even more consequential was Murie's observation that wolves and their prey existed in rough parity, the concept later popularized as the "balance of nature." Murie perceived that wolves couldn't kill ungulates at will. He saw that they targeted the sick and aged, and understood why. Murie determined that wolves were a major source of mortality for Mount McKinley Park sheep and yet argued that the two species were currently in balance.

Murie's five years of unprejudiced observation of wolves in Mount McKinley Park transformed the way educated people understand wolves and other predators. Murie's views were controversial in his day, which shouldn't be surprising. What is remarkable is how controversial those perceptions remain today. People still fight about wolf impacts on ungulate populations.

Above all, people fight about this in the state where Murie did his pioneering work, Alaska.

A world apart

It is difficult for non-Alaskans to understand Alaska. Twice the size of Texas, Alaska is populated by fewer humans than live in the state of Rhode Island or the province of Quebec. While the south-central region has a few roads, the vast interior is essentially wilderness. Only 20 percent of the state can be reached by road.

Alaskans are as unique as their homeland. Many moved to Alaska specifically to get away from the nettlesome restraints of civilization and to live in a beautiful, wild country. Alaskans typically have a strong emotional attachment to the natural world, but it is far less sentimental and more utilitarian than is common in the Lower 48 states.

One consequence of Alaska's extreme separation from the rest of the US is a fierce sense of independence. Alaskans are fed up with the many ways outsiders misunderstand them, and they balk when outsiders tell them how they are to conduct their affairs.

Alaskan attitudes about hunting are different, too. Alaskans hunt and fish at higher rates than the citizens of any other state in the US.

The wolf was never endangered in Alaska, but harsh management has impacted numbers at times in the past.

Alaskans have the expectation that, when they need meat, they should be able to walk out somewhere reasonably nearby and shoot a moose. Harvesting one's own meat is a cherished tradition among Alaska's people, the white residents no less than the indigenous peoples.

Outsiders are also likely to misunderstand the Alaskan attitude toward wolves. Few states of the Lower 48 have wolves, and those that do still tend to think of them as a persecuted endangered species. People in the Lower 48 equate killing wolves with wolf hatred.

That's just not an issue in Alaska. Alaskans love wolves. With very few exceptions, Alaskans all agree that wolves are wonderful and they are proud to have so many living in the state. And yet appreciating wolves doesn't mean that Alaskans aren't ready to have quite a few of them killed if there seems to be a good reason for it.

The wolves of Alaska

As is true in Canada, wolves are anything but endangered in Alaska. They occur almost everywhere throughout the mainland. Wolves are also found on Unimak Island in the Aleutians, and on all major southeastern islands except Admiralty, Baranof, and Chichagof. Putting it another way, 85 percent of today's Alaska is wolf country. Wolf densities are lowest in the rainforest of the panhandle and on the arctic plains north of the Brooks Range.

Alaska's Department of Fish and Game (ADFG) doesn't count its wolf population nose-by-nose as game departments in the Lower 48 do, but the agency does track population trends. The department estimates the population at 7,000 to 11,200 wolves, more or less where it has been for years. Researchers believe that the state's wolf population is holding steady or increasing slightly. In the words of one Alaska manager, "On planet Earth, this is *the* stronghold for wolves."

Alaska has two kinds of wolf, both subtypes of the gray wolf. The dominant wolf, in all

senses, is *Canis lupus occidentalis*, the wolf known in Canada as the Mackenzie Valley wolf and in some parts of the US as the Rocky Mountain wolf. It might be better to call it the Northwest wolf, as modern texts are beginning to do. This is the wolf found almost everywhere in Alaska except the rainforest of the southeast.

The Northwest wolf is a big, rugged wolf. Adult male wolves typically weigh 85 to 115 pounds (38 to 53 kg). An occasional big male will push the scales to 145 pounds (65 kg), or even a bit more. Females run a bit smaller.

Pelt color varies all the way from almost white to black. The wolves of Alaska don't have as much brown, red, or cream as in their coats as gray wolves elsewhere. Gray and black are the most common colors. Alaska does not have the arctic subtype of wolf that exists in the arctic regions of Canada.

Alaska's second wolf is the Alexander Archipelago wolf. This is a small, black wolf found in the rainforest of the panhandle in the Tongass National Forest. The Alexander Archipelago wolf is highly distinct and not very numerous. The most recent estimate puts the population at about 900 wolves. We'll learn more about this wolf later.

Moose and caribou are by far the most important prey items for Alaska's wolves. They take Dall sheep in certain regions. In southeastern Alaska, the wolves' diet includes Sitka black-tailed deer and mountain goats. In appropriate habitat, especially in summer, beaver become an important food item. Wolves will scrounge almost anything in summer, including hares, squirrels, birds, and even lemmings. Alexander Archipelago wolves also eat salmon when the fish are swarming upstream to spawn in such massive concentrations that the wolves can catch them.

Most Alaskan wolves defend territory in the normal way, with the territories being very large in some areas because the prey density is so low. A mean average territory size is 600 square miles (1000 square km^2). Wolves in deer-rich Minnesota, by contrast, might maintain territories that are one tenth as large. Alaska has a lot of wolves, but it is a tough place for a wolf to make a living.

Some Alaskan wolves have a lifestyle based on caribou. Caribou migrate, so these wolves travel with the caribou herds rather than denning and defending a defined territory.

Researchers have long noted that wolves of northern climates run in larger packs. Alaska's wolf packs typically have six to seven wolves, but packs of 20 or even 30 animals are not unknown. Until recently, researchers assumed large packs were necessary to take down such formidable prey as moose. But the real killing is often done by two or three wolves, with others just watching. It now seems that large packs are favored because that allows wolves to make the most efficient use of their kills.

Historical perspectives

Wolves were persecuted in Alaska as ruthlessly as elsewhere, although they never were close to extirpation. There was too much land, too much brush, too many wolves, and too few people to wipe out all the wolves.

Things changed with the availability of small airplanes after World War II. Before airplanes made it so easy to travel to remote areas, wolves living any distance from humans were safe. People quickly learned how easy it was to spot wolves against the snow from airplanes, and then they learned they could chase wolves with airplanes and shoot them. A new sport was born. Some hunters enjoyed aerial wolf hunting because it was exciting and produced valuable pelts. Alaska's managers were happy to have people shooting wolves because that meant they didn't have to do it. Everyone assumed killing wolves would increase numbers of moose and caribou.

A 1955 article in *Field & Stream* called "Strafing Arctic Killers" described this new type of hunting. The author congratulates himself for killing wolves because that would make more food available for "Eskimos," although it is un-

likely that the hunter really felt he was doing community service as he gunned wolves in the snow.

The 1950s were especially rough on wolves. Federal authorities undertook a vigorous campaign against them that combined poison, traps, snares, and aerial gunning. A bounty offered additional incentives for private citizens to take wolves.

That all changed in 1959, the year Alaska achieved statehood. The new Alaska Department of Fish and Game (ADFG) was staffed by professionally trained wildlife managers. The ADFG was proud to put in place enlightened, predator-friendly wolf policies. Managers dropped the use of poison and repealed the bounties. The department classified wolves as a big game animal and managed them as a renewable resource.

Aerial gunning of wolves became more and more popular in the 1960s, but the practice became controversial. There is something unsettling about the image of hunters in an airplane pursuing wolves in heavy snow until they are so exhausted they can be shot. The advantages of technology are so overwhelming that this form of hunting looks cruel and unfair. Many people felt so, and in 1971, the US Congress passed the Federal Airborne Hunting Act, making this kind of sport hunting illegal. The ADFG quit issuing aerial hunting permits.

Ungulate decline

At about that time, a series of exceptionally severe winters hit moose and caribou herds. Wolves began rebuilding their numbers as moose and caribou numbers plummeted to dangerously low levels. Wolves were not the only reason for failing ungulate numbers. Severe weather and predation by bears were two of several factors pushing ungulate numbers down.

New research, much of it done in Alaska, began suggesting that predation can depress ungulate populations. Any intellectual system is subject to periodic swings of opinion, and so

Wolves thrive in Alaska, but prey density is low and wolves often must hunt a large territory to survive.

it is with thinking about the impact wolves can have on ungulates. Researchers originally sought to refute hysterical claims that wolves "wipe out" ungulate populations. Research emphasized the comforting lesson that there is a "balance of nature" that keeps predators and prey in balance.

Newer research began to complicate that picture by showing that an ungulate population in trouble could be kept at low levels by predation. Wolves do mainly take ungulates that are sick, injured, old, or otherwise compromised. But wolves and bears prey heavily on young ungulates, the moose and caribou calves that represent the future for their kind. Researchers began reporting that wolves limit ungulate populations, and they were saying this just when political pressures were mounting for the ADFG to "do something" to help failing moose and caribou herds. The pendulum of opinion swung against wolves.

Starting in 1975, ADFG began running wolf control programs – killing wolves – in particular regions where moose or caribou were not doing well. The policy was generally popular in Alaska with people who wanted more moose and caribou, but even some Alaskans were outraged by what seemed like a return to discredited wolf-management practices of the past.

Wolf wars

Pro-wolf and animal rights groups began suing the ADFG, hoping to stop what they saw as an unjustifiable "slaughter" of wolves. To them, this was classic wolf hatred with a new face. The wolf was just acquiring its new identity as a persecuted endangered species in the Lower 48. Seen in that context, Alaska's eagerness to kill hundreds of wolves seemed outrageous. Most critics ignored the ADFG rationale for reducing wolf numbers. Others concluded that building ungulate numbers by killing so many wolves was obscene, never mind the rationale.

Thus began Alaska's wolf wars. Pro-wolf, animal rights, and environmental groups began dragging the ADFG into court over and over again. As the legal wrangling went on, each side grew increasingly disgusted with the other. Alaskans bristled at what they saw as arrogant and uninformed meddling from outsiders who wanted to turn Alaska into "one big park." Alaska's critics decided the whole state lacked ecological sensitivity, and they were contemptuous of the scientific research coming out of Alaska that defended wolf control.

Alaska's wolf war became front-page news in 1992 when the ADFG announced its plans to remove a high percentage of wolves from several management units. Environmental groups reacted to the proposed wolf killing by declaring a tourist boycott of Alaska. Governor Wally Hickel received over 100,000 letters critical of

Alaskans love wolves, but many Alaskans favor wolf control to improve ungulate populations.

his wolf policies, and Alaska found itself cast in an unflattering light on television news shows. In the face of this firestorm, Hickel backed down and announced a delay on wolf control, but the issue remained unresolved.

Over the years, changes in the governor's office have affected wolf management. Hickel, the strong wolf-control advocate, had two widely separated terms, from 1966 to 1969 and 1990 to 1994. Governor Steve Cowper (1986 to 1990) prohibited wolf control during his term. Governor Tony Knowles (1994 to 2002) was elected at a time when Alaska was taking a beating in the media for its wolf program. Knowles shelved wolf control with the exception of one nonlethal project. Frank Murkowski, elected in 2002, seems eager to resume intensive wolf control.

A more recent effort at tourist boycott failed to catch hold. Legal battles show no sign of abating.

Land and shoot

A mostly separate and equally contentious debate has raged over "land-and-shoot" aerial hunting. The 1972 Airborne Hunting Act made it illegal for hunters to haze, herd, drive, harass, or shoot animals from airplanes. But after the act was passed, it still remained legal to spot a pack of wolves from the air, land an airplane nearby, jump out, and shoot a wolf.

The sport became increasingly controversial. Critics believed land-and-shoot hunters routinely violated the rules by shooting wolves from the air or by running them to exhaustion and then shooting them as they lay panting in the snow. Since aerial hunting took place in remote country with no witnesses, there was no practicable way to enforce regulations on land and shoot. The symbolism of hunters killing wolves from airplanes continued to disgust many people, including many avid hunters who feel land-and-shoot hunting violates all the traditions of a "fair chase."

In spite of negative publicity, the ADFG continued to defend land-and-shoot wolf hunting.

The department might have stuck with land and shoot so stubbornly because eliminating the use of airplanes would have deprived it of any way to run an effective hunting season on wolves. In a large state with virtually no roads, airplanes offered practically the only way to hunt wolves.

The land-and-shoot controversy carried on for years and gave the ADFG a black eye by making the department look insensitive. Environmentalists seized on this issue as proof that the department could not be trusted.

The controversy seemed to be settled in 1996 when Alaskans passed a ballot initiative that made land and shoot illegal, specifically mandating that a hunter could not shoot a wolf on the same day as flying. The measure was approved by 59 percent of Alaska voters.

That would seem to be the end of the story, and yet in 1999 the state legislature brought land and shoot back. Legislators passed a bill that would allow land-and-shoot hunting in specific game management areas where the ADFG wanted wolf numbers dropped. The bill was vetoed by Governor Knowles. The legislature passed it again, overriding the veto.

Then the whole state spoke up again in 2000. In a second general initiative vote, 53 percent of Alaskans rejected land-and-shoot hunting.

In the latest twist, ADFG has authorized aerial wolf control to be done by private parties. Critics call this a resurrection of land and shoot, since private individuals will be killing wolves from the air. The department counters that this is just a departmental wolf-control project that they are, in effect, subcontracting.

Wolf control

It is a primary responsibility of the ADFG to maintain healthy ungulate populations. In fact, the state's charter mandates the department to keep moose and caribou populations at strong levels for the benefit of all Alaskans. People who feel ungulate numbers are too low in their area – and that would be many

Alaskans – put pressure on ADFG to shoot wolves because wolf control seems like the quickest and least expensive way to boost ungulate numbers.

Alaska's managers stoutly defend their wolf control programs as being based on science. The ADFG has conducted multiple research programs that leave it convinced wolf control is a valid management technique. Researchers for the ADFG claim that any time an ungulate population falls to a low level, for whatever reason, wolves and other predators can keep it pinned low for many years. The department coined a phrase for this: The ungulates were caught in a "predator pit."

Some of that research suggests that Alaska had a special problem with multiple predators. In many areas of the state, predators include black bears, grizzly bears, and wolves. If predators take more than 90 percent of the young – as they did in some studies – caribou numbers get locked in at low levels. Moose are even more vulnerable. Typically, 100 cow moose give birth to about 120 to 140 calves each year. In some studies, predators whittled that cohort to just 10 to 20 survivors at summer's end. Moose cannot sustain populations while losing that many young to predators each year.

One reason the ADFG has turned to killing wolves is a lack of managerial options. The vast size of Alaska and the lack of roads make travel very expensive. Managers can indirectly affect habitat quality by allowing some fires to burn. If ungulate numbers drop too far, managers can cut back on the hunters' harvest, but this is obviously unpopular. And managers can increase the take of predators by relaxing trapping and hunting limits, yet this often has limited effect.

Research points to bear predation as being very significant on young moose. So why concentrate predator control on wolves when bears are a major part of the problem? Because bears are a long-lived species with low fertility. If managers were to goof and take too many bears from an area, bear numbers would be low

for a long time. Wolves, with their great fertility, can bounce back quickly.

The review
In 1994, at the peak of ugly publicity about wolf control, recently elected governor Tony Knowles suspended all control plans and called for a National Academy of Sciences review of Alaska's wolf program.

The report, published in 1997, disappointed partisans on both sides. The committee found that predator-prey relationships are complex to study and difficult to manipulate. The scientific panel praised the ADFG for its ambitious research, and then went on to say that those studies did not make a compelling case for wolf control. The panel's economic analysis also made it clear that it is very difficult to justify the expense of wolf control.

The panel noted that in only three of eleven cases did ungulate populations respond favorably to wolf-control actions. That means wolf control sometimes works; it also means that it often doesn't work. The panel concluded that many wolf-control actions had not been backed up with good scientific data.

The ADFG has maintained for years that there are two possible stable predator-prey situations. One, which might be the one most often found in nature, has both predators and prey present in low numbers. The other has both predator and prey species present in high numbers. Managers have described that second condition as the ideal toward which their wolf-control measures are aimed. The review panel, however, dismissed that goal as "not justified" by data.

For wolf control to be effective, a great many wolves have to die. The committee found that wolf control has resulted in prey increases only when wolf numbers were seriously reduced over a large area for at least four years. Wolves can sustain an annual harvest of 20 to 40 percent without declining in population, which means that wolf control doesn't work unless a high percentage of the wolves are killed. Wolf-

Some researchers believe the future of wolf management might feature economical, effective ways of limiting wolf fertility (rather than killing wolves).

control actions typically try to remove 80 percent of the wolves in an area. After wolf control stops, the wolves usually come back at pre-control levels in two to five years.

That does not guarantee a favorable response in ungulate numbers. Increasingly, biologists question whether the financial and social price of so much killing makes sense.

The Knowles administration decided it would proceed with wolf control in specific management areas only if three conditions were met. The action had to be based on sound science, it had to be cost-effective, and it had to have broad public acceptance.

It is hard to say what Alaska's policies will be in the future. The current governor, Frank Murkowski, is much more enthusiastic about wolf control than his predecessor. The ADFG has authorized some wolf-control projects, but only on 5 percent of the state's territory.

The issue of the efficacy of wolf control is complex. Not all research points in the same direction. What seems increasingly clear is that a management program that was acceptable half a century ago is becoming increasingly unacceptable today, although it remains popular with many Alaskans.

Dink wolves

Although the Knowles administration did not want to pursue lethal wolf control, it faced a critical situation with one of Alaska's famous

CHAPTER 13

The Wolves of Canada: Holding Their Own

Canada, an immense land with almost unimaginable variety, is as large as the US but has only a tenth of the human population. Since humans are concentrated in southern and coastal cities, there are vast stretches of Canada where wolves are born, live, and die with little or no contact with people. With a total of about 56,000 animals, Canada is home to more wolves than any other nation on Earth.

Wolves originally occurred almost everywhere, from coast to coast to as far north as Ellesmere Island (see page 141). Apparently, there never were wolves on Prince Edward Island, Anticosti Island, and the Queen Charlotte Islands. Europeans extirpated wolves from some areas, including New Brunswick, Nova Scotia, Newfoundland, the highly settled portions of Quebec, Ontario, and the western provinces. Even so, wolves today still occupy 85 percent of their original range in Canada. So wolf management in Canada is unique.

Historical perspective

The history of wolf management in Canada parallels the story in the US. That should not be surprising. Both countries were developed at the same time, both being settled by European immigrants who feared wolves. Settlement in both cases started on the east coast and rolled west. In Canada as in the US, settlers assumed wolf eradication was a necessary step in the process of making an untamed land productive and making the world safe for wild and domesticated ungulates.

Upon unpacking their bags in the New World, Europeans emigrants began eradicating wolves. Of course, the first source of profit in Canada was the fur industry, so wolves were trapped for their luxurious pelts. Quebec and Ontario already offered bounties by 1793. Wolves became rare in the eastern provinces by 1870. They were gone from New Brunswick by 1880, from Nova Scotia by 1900, and from Newfoundland by 1913.

The first travelers to the Great Plains were awed by bison herds that reached from one horizon to the other. In 1754, Anthony Henday recorded seeing "Wolves without number . . . I cannot say whether the wolves or the buffalo are more numerous." Not much more than a century later, market hunting had already wiped out the great herds as well as the elk, antelope, and deer that formerly grazed on the grassy prairies. With very little natural prey available, wolves in prairie regions turned to livestock. Alberta and Saskatchewan set up bounties in 1899, followed a year later by British Columbia.

"Wolfing" was a lucrative occupation as well as an infamous lifestyle. By combining incomes from pelts and bounties, wolfers could earn the modern equivalent of US$40,000 in a year. The tools of the trade were traps, strychnine, and dynamite. In 1873, a dispute over some missing horses led a group of wolfers to murder 30 Assiniboine Indians. This incident demonstrated the need for more law in remote regions and directly led to the creation of the Northwest Mounted Police. Canadians telling this story usually mention that the killers were Americans, although wolfers were a rough lot in general and supposedly reeked even worse than buffalo hunters.

Wolf extirpation continued through the early decades of the 20th century, although many wolves were protected by living in remote places. Low pelt prices in the 1940s reduced pressure on wolves, and they rebounded in some areas. That was sharply reversed when the sudden abundance of small airplanes after World War II led to aerial hunting. The 1950s also saw a return of poisoning programs intended to increase game populations popular with sport hunters. Some cite 1955 as the peak year of what can only be described as carnage. Wolf hunters used airplanes to service bait stations all over remote areas. There was a lot of collateral damage in the form of unintended victims.

Wolves got relief in the mid-1960s and 1970s when professionally educated wildlife managers assumed positions of responsibility in game agencies. These men had been trained in the science of ecology and the recently invented profession of game management. Unlike their agriculture-school-educated predecessors, these managers understood that predator species are vital members of a larger, interconnected ecological community. The appearance in 1963 of Farley Mowat's *Never Cry Wolf* was both a cause and an expression of a new perception of wolves. This was the first positive representation of wolves in popular culture. The book was widely read in Canada, as its author was Canadian. Increasingly, Canadian wildlife managers adopted a more tolerant view of wolves.

Canada produced one of the early giants of wolf research in Douglas Pimlott. Pimlott perfected the art of locating wolves by howling and did important early work on the wolves of Algonquin Park. Reflecting in the 1970s on the long history of wolf persecution, Pimlott mused, "Will the species still exist when the 20th century passes into history?" The answer was not clear. Given the history of men and wolves, it seemed quite likely to Pimlott that wolves would join passenger pigeons and dodos as museum exhibits.

Canada now has a strong cadre of talented researchers dedicated to managing wolves wisely. The managers and administrators whom they advise are professional enough to mean well, although some operate in political environments that make wise wolf management difficult. Wildlife managers are under constant pressure to improve populations of moose, caribou, elk, and deer. One of the most popular ways to do that is wolf control – killing wolves in the hope that local ungulate populations will rise. The technique rarely pays off as well as proponents predict, but wolf control is a preferred nostrum with hunting groups, and it is their license fees that fund much game management. Still, Canadian managers have not practiced wolf control lately on a scale sufficient to do significant damage to overall wolf numbers.

Canadian wolf and wildlife management in recent decades has had high and low moments. Many of the nation's wolves continue to live natural lives, largely isolated from guns, traps, and snares. But when the interests of wolves come into conflict with some other economic interest, such as logging or ranching, wolves almost always lose.

The wolves of Canada

Most authorities think Canada has five gray wolf subtypes – four, if taxonomists conclude that the smallish wolf of eastern Ontario and Quebec is not a gray wolf.

The wolf of the far north is *Canis lupus arctos*, the arctic wolf. These are large wolves with several adaptations for life in extreme cold: their coats are creamy white, their muzzles and legs are short, and their ears are more rounded. Arctic wolves mostly live above the latitude of 67° north. On Ellesmere Island, they principally feed upon musk oxen, a formidable prey. Low prey density forces arctic wolves to hunt territories larger than 1,000 square miles (2,600 km²). On the Queen Elizabeth Islands, some arctic wolves scavenge seal kills from polar bears and might have learned to hunt seals for themselves.

The wolf of the western provinces is *Canis lupus occidentalis*, often called the Mackenzie Valley wolf, but now more often known in scientific texts as the Northwest wolf. It is a large wolf, with some males weighing 145 pounds (66 kg). In the Northwest Territories and elsewhere, some of these wolves have evolved a nomadic lifestyle, traveling more or less constantly with caribou herds rather than denning and defending a home territory.

The wolf found in western Ontario, northern Quebec, and around both shores of Hudson's Bay is *Canis lupus nubilis*, the Great Plains wolf. This is the very widespread gray wolf that is also found in the Great Lakes region. The original range of this wolf included parts of British Columbia.

Some authorities believe the wolf of coastal British Columbia deserves its own name because it is distinct. The relatively small, rust- and ochre-colored wolf is sometimes called *Canis lupus fuscus*, the "coastal wolf." It is possibly a regional variant of the *nubilis* wolf. Studies show it is genetically distinct from inland wolves. This coastal wolf hunts black-tailed deer and has developed proficiency at catching migrating salmon, often eating only the head. Coastal wolves have coarse hair to help shed water. They readily swim long distances between the shore and islands in search of prey.

The wolf of Quebec and the eastern half of Ontario is *Canis lupus lycaon*, often called the "eastern wolf," "timber wolf," or "eastern Canada wolf." As we've noted earlier, the taxonomic status of this wolf is in doubt. Some researchers think of this as *Canis lycaon*, which is to say they don't regard it as a gray wolf but rather a member of the wolf family that is much closer to the red wolf than to gray wolves, possibly even the same wolf. Compared to the gray wolf, the eastern wolf is smaller, with longer legs, a narrow snout, eyes spaced farther apart, and ears large for its head. The eastern wolf has tawny legs and face, a salt-and-pepper coat, and cinnamon behind the ears. The most famous members of this group are the highly studied wolves of Algonquin Park. A variant of this wolf with some distinctive qualities is found in Quebec's Laurentide Reserve. These wolves mostly prey upon deer, beavers, and moose.

Provincial issues

Each province or territory's wolf population faces unique issues and circumstances.

Yukon Territory: The Yukon is one of the least developed areas of North America. Human population density in a recent year was one person per 10 square kilometers (3.8 mi²). The estimated wolf population is 4,500. The annual human take is only about 200 and is conducted mostly by native hunters. Wolves preying on the Porcupine caribou herd travel with it as it migrates. Packs in the Yukon that defend territories instead must hunt large areas because of low prey density.

Northwest Territories and Nunavat: This

immense wilderness is larger than many countries. The geography is varied, including mountains, river valleys, muskeg, and tundra. Travel is almost exclusively by airplane, and the human population density is even lower than in the Yukon. The wolf population is estimated at 10,000 and is considered stable. This region has arctic wolves in the north and Mackenzie Valley wolves in the south. Wolves living below the tree line or in mountains mostly hunt nonmigrating prey such as moose and bison. They defend territories in the way of most wolves. Wolves living on the arctic islands prey on caribou, musk ox, and arctic hares. A third group lives above the tree line on the mainland, and these wolves mostly migrate with caribou herds.

British Columbia: Habitat in British Columbia varies from the sodden coastal rainforest to the rugged Rocky Mountains. The overall wolf population is estimated at 8,000 and might be increasing. Yet there are trouble spots. On Vancouver Island, industrial-scale, clear-cut logging is altering the face of the land. Black-tailed deer numbers are falling, and the Vancouver Island marmot, another food source, is endangered. In spite of evidence pointing to logging as the cause, managers propose to kill wolves and cougars to aid deer and marmots. Logging also threatens the coastal wolf, which might be genetically distinct enough to warrant special protection. Apart from that, British Columbia wolves are prospering. The annual take by hunters, 750 wolves, is too small to have any impact.

Alberta: Since Alberta is highly settled in the agricultural south, sparsely settled in the north, wolves are increasing in the north, possibly decreasing in the south. Overall numbers are estimated at about 4,200 wolves.

There is concern in Alberta for specific populations, such as the Banff National Park wolves, down to only 25. Parks such as Banff, Kootenay, and Yoyo provide protection to wolves, but only so long as they stay in the parks. Those that stray outside often die, as

there is no love for wolves among ranchers surrounding the parks. The Trans-Canada Highway and Canadian Pacific Railway transect two of the province's national parks. Spilled grain from railway cars lures elk and deer to the tracks, prey that in turn attracts wolves. That results in many dead wolves.

One group of wolves in Alberta's Wood Buffalo National Park lives almost exclusively on bison, the last wolves on Earth to do so. Bison are one of the most dangerous prey species hunted by wolves. The wolves of Yellowstone, surrounded by bison, avoid them and hunt elk instead.

Alberta contributed the wolves for the initial Yellowstone translocation. Those wolves were captured just east of Jasper Park. Wolves in that region are killed at rates approaching 40 percent annually, and yet populations are holding. They have to be reckoned the luckiest wolves that ever lived, going from a place rich with wolf traps to a place rich with naïve elk.

Provincial managers do not seem to make wolves much of a priority, and yet the overall picture is of a strong population that might be increasing slightly.

Saskatchewan: This province estimates it has 4,300 wolves. The relatively minor human take does not adversely impact the population. The province is divided into two regions: the agricultural Interior Plains region and the Canadian Shield, a rocky region pocked with lakes and covered with a coniferous forest. Wolves are found mostly in the northern forests.

Manitoba: Wolves were mostly extirpated from agricultural regions in the 1870s. Today wolves are primarily restricted to the boreal forests and tundra regions of the province. In the southern agricultural area, segregated populations occur in islands of habitat including Riding Mountain National Park and Duck Mountain Provincial Forest. A small population might exist in the Spruce Woods Provincial Park/Shilo Military Base Forest. Wolves also commonly occur in agricultural fringe areas bordering Sandilands and Agassiz

Provincial Forests, the Interlake, and Westlake areas. Wolves occur in 50 percent of the province.

Manitoba's wolf population numbers approximately 4,000 to 6,000 and appears to be stable. An exception is the Riding Mountain population, which has recently decreased. In response to this decline, wolf hunting has been curtailed around the Riding Mountain. There currently is strong public support for protecting this population, which is quite isolated and may be genetically unique.

The general policy in Manitoba is to allow wolf numbers to rise or fall on their own, although wolf control actions are taken in specific areas where wolves are causing trouble for farmers or ranchers, and wolves are sometimes removed in northern areas when native communities complain about their impacts on ungulates.

Ontario: Ontario is home to an estimated 9,000 wolves, a population that seems to be

The vast, lightly populated expanse of Canada has helped maintain wolf populations across the whole country. In contrast, the US programs support recovery in relatively limited, isolated areas.

Occupied wolf range

Occupied recovery area

Historical wolf range

Potential recovery area

Potential area for study

Map drawn from Equator Graphics'
map for Defenders of Wildlife.

stable. Wolves are found in 80 percent of their original range, having lost habitat in some highly developed southern areas. Several hundred wolves are taken each year by trappers and hunters, mostly trappers, but not enough to affect the overall numbers. Habitat loss and fragmentation is probably more of a threat. For example, a logging road planned to run through part of the Pukasaw Provincial Park might cut a path through the territories of four wolf packs.

There has been much concern in Ontario and beyond about the long-range future of the famous wolves of Algonquin Park, Canada's oldest and most beloved park. Wolves here are a big draw. By 2002, 116,000 visitors had participated in its howling programs. Researchers John and Mary Theberge have argued that the park's wolves are dying at unsustainable rates when they leave the park. Not all researchers agree, but there was enough evidence of trouble to cause provincial authorities to create a safety zone around the park where wolves can travel in safety. Even if it is a symbolic victory, the symbolism is encouraging. Earlier, park officials became alarmed by a series of aggressive incidents involving bold, habituated wolves. They now have a policy of removing wolves that seem too comfortable around humans.

Future plans for Algonquin might involve interesting ecological judgments. The original wolf of the area was probably the gray wolf, just as the original prey was moose and caribou. After logging altered the habitat, deer replaced moose and caribou and the more delicate *lycaon* replaced the gray wolf . . . or at least that is one theory. Now the habitat is aging in ways that favor moose and deer.

Quebec: The wolf of Quebec is *Canis lupus lycaon*, the eastern wolf or eastern Canada wolf. The province has an estimated 6,000 wolves, many of them in protected parks or reserves. One of the most intriguing wolf populations is based in the Laurentide Reserve. Trapping is apparently allowed in the park. These wolves are thought to be prime candidates to repopulate wolfless habitat in the northeastern US. The population is probably increasing.

Labrador: The population is about 2,000 wolves. Each year trappers take a small number of them.

Toward the future

Some challenges lie ahead for wolf populations in Canada. The problem of wolves on Vancouver Island is emblematic. The endangered marmots surely need some help, but it is far from sure that killing wolves is the right response.

Similarly, in the Northwest Territories, the high arctic population of Peary Caribou is endangered. The arctic wolf that preys on them is part of the problem, and yet that wolf population itself has low numbers right now. Managers will have to make some difficult choices to give both species a chance to restore themselves. Another possible concern is open-pit diamond mining in remote the remote tundra of Northwest Territories, which is bringing about changes that are likely to work against caribou and wolves. If economic development is coming only now to northern Canada, it nevertheless is coming.

Some of the central and western provinces might need to think about creating protected zones where wolves can move in and out of parks. Habitat fragmentation continues to be a threat, and the wolves of Banff are an example of a dangerously isolated group in a place where high visitor interest might argue for more intensive management.

The recent decision in Ontario to protect wolves in the ring around Algonquin would look like progress. What might mean more in the long run is the thorough review Ontario is now doing of its wolf program. Provincial managers want to come up with a comprehensive plan that will balance the interests of wolves with all other interests.

Plans of this sort are not common in Canada, as managers have up until now had the luxury of not worrying much about wolves. After

The wolf of Algonquin Park, often called the Canada or Eastern wolf, has just received important protection in the perimeter of the park.

the provinces dropped aggressive predator control programs, they have been able to take strong wolf populations for granted. Wolves have done well because they have been protected by their isolation from people with traps, guns, and snares. That isolation, in turn, has been based on the fact people haven't found many ways to make money from Canada's vast stretches of muskeg, tundra, and other wild lands. It is significant that the most populous province is now developing a modern, comprehensive plan designed to ensure that Ontario's wolves have a place in ecosystem of the future.

Other provinces might need to do the same kind of planning. An observer recently noted, "Canada has done all the same things to its wolves that we have in the US, just a little later and not nearly as completely." Development is coming late to remote lands that were of more use to wolves than humans. But it is coming. Sooner or later, balances will need to be struck between the interests of wolves and the interests of humans.

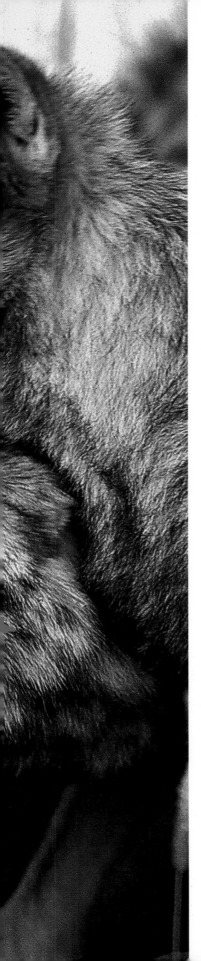

CHAPTER 14

What Future for Wolves?

Predicting the future of wolves in North America is a hazardous enterprise. Nobody could have predicted the great reversal in public perception that made wolf restoration possible. The wisest observers of wolf politics, in fact, assumed wolves would disappear from the wild. Such men as Aldo Leopold, Adolph Murie, and Douglas Pimlott often spoke as if wolf eradication would continue until no wolves would live outside of zoos.

Those thoughtful men did not come close to forecasting what happened in North America between 1970 and 2000. They never imagined that a law protecting endangered species would have the power to restore the most controversial animal on the North American continent.

Even less could Leopold, Murie, or Pimlott have anticipated a time when wolves would be actually revered by many people. Imagine their astonishment if they could visit Yellowstone today and see wolf tourists racing up and down the Lamar Valley Road with spotting scopes, cheering at the sight of wolves taking down an elk.

If such wise men were unable to see into the future, only a bold fool would now claim to know what the relationship between wolves and humans might be in several decades. Even so, it is surely worthwhile to make the effort.

Wolf education

Wolf education – teaching people about wolves – is a young field. Some observers regard Minnesota naturalist Sigurd Olsen the earliest wolf educator. Olsen tracked wolves in the snow in the 1930s to learn more about them. Others say that the first objective observation of wolves happened when Adolph Murie recorded the daily activities of the East Fork Pack in 1939. Olsen and Murie were gifted writers who produced entertaining accounts of their wolf research. And yet both remained obscure outside scientific circles until much later.

A strong case can be made that modern wolf education began when Dave Mech gave the world his first great book, *The Wolf*, in 1970. Although written for students and fellow scientists, this book struck a chord with the general public. Mech is a remarkable man who combines enthusiasm for wolves with the disciplined mind of a scientist.

*While public perceptions of wolves have changed to a startling degree, that doesn't guarantee future toler-
ance. The need for wolf education continues.*

The Wolf set in motion a stunning change in
public perception of wolves.

Many factors combined to advance the wolf
education movement. For example, urbaniza-
tion meant that fewer people actually stood to
lose cattle or sheep to wolves. For North Americans living in cities, wolves are a beguiling idea
rather than any kind of threat.

Similarly, people increasingly acquire their
notions about wolves from the media, especially television. Wolves film well. Their ath-
leticism and intelligence make wolves natural
video stars. The affection wolves exhibit toward pups and other pack members is very appealing.

The environmental movement helped shape
a new public image of wolves. In the social tur-
bulence of the late 1960s and early 1970s, environmentalism arose as a new way of looking

at "nature" and man. One of its first accomplishments was rehabilitating the sullied
image of predators. Environmentalism soon
became a potent political force.

The crowning achievement of the environmental movement was passage of the Endangered Species Act (ESA). Because the act was
meant to prevent the ultimate biological
tragedy – the eternal loss of animal species –
it was exceptionally powerful. Wolves were almost the first animals placed on the list of
species in peril. That gave wolves an identity
totally at odds with their ancient reputation.
An animal previously considered the most
scurrilous villain of the animal kingdom was
redefined as the most unfairly persecuted
species in history.

Many people – especially children – draw
their images of animals from books. In the

years following the listing of the wolf as an endangered species, the image of wolves in children's books was reversed. The slavering beast that gobbled Granny in "Little Red Riding Hood" became the sympathetic, family-friendly animal of such books as Melinda Julietta's *We Are Wolves,* in which an uncle wolf teaches some pups what it takes to be a wolf.

This transformation was promoted through the creation of a new type of education, environmental education. Naturalists drafted environmental curricula for schools and colleges. Some state legislatures mandated that schools teach the principles of ecology. Environmental education was promoted through a network of nature centers, parks, and environmental learning centers. Ontario's Algonquin Park, to note just one example, has exposed thousands of visitors to the mystique of wolves.

Wolves themselves provided some of the great stars of the wolf education movement. Ambassador wolves are pen-raised wolves that are habituated to people. Wolf educators took these friendly wolves into school classrooms, legislative halls, and other places where people could admire their beauty and dignity. The contrast between these amiable ambassadors and the horrible old stereotypes converted people into wolf advocates.

Wolf advocacy and environmental groups did wonderful work to educate the public to new realities about wolves. With the rise of the Internet, groups had a new way to disseminate their wolf-friendly message.

Between 1970 and 2000, the most vilified animal on the continent became the poster child for the ESA and a cause célèbre. To my knowledge, no comparable shift in public perception of an animal species has ever happened.

A new image

Social scientists have been fascinated by this. Students of public opinion have used surveys to plot the great swing in perceptions of the wolf. While each survey is a little different, all now document general public acceptance of wolves. Typically, 70 percent of those polled have strongly positive views of wolves. While people disagree about just how many wolves are desirable and how they should be managed, the surveys make it clear that people love wolves and want some in the wild.

A better indicator of the new image of wolves might be the political power of wolf advocates. In spite of frenzied opposition from the livestock industry, wolves have triumphed in court contests time after time. Those victories were made possible by the muscle of the ESA but they also represented the great will of all the people who were determined to restore wolves.

These victories weren't all the result of public relations. Wolf advocates had a huge advantage over wolf opponents in these wolf wars, namely the weight of scientific evidence. When wolf advocates claimed that wolves would not decimate ungulate populations, for example, they were right. It doesn't hurt to be right if you are in a political or legal battle. That is never enough, but it helps.

The changing message

Early wolf educators had a simple and attractive task. They had to combat ignorance and prejudice. Their most potent weapon was the truth. Wolf educators enjoyed debunking irrational wolf hatred, especially all the loony myths about wolves that arose in medieval Europe. It was a joyful time to be an environmental educator because it feels good to deliver a positive message about a misunderstood species.

As people began seeing wolves in a new way, wolf educators found their work was becoming more complicated. Some pro-wolf groups and individuals became strident in their wolf advocacy. Wolf fans sometimes spoke as if wolves are saints that behave more nobly than most human beings. Wolf educators increasingly found themselves caught between irrational wolf hatred and irrational wolf adoration.

At a symposium on wolves, I met a man

whose professional life had largely consisted of defending wolves. He had frequently faced hostile audiences of deer hunters and farmers who "knew" wolves would wreak havoc if restored. This man had just emerged from a meeting in which he found himself under assault from wolf advocates. "Two hours ago I thought I loved wolves," he mused. "But I just learned I am a wolf-hater who is drenched in blood because I think that those wolves that attack livestock should be removed."

Wolf educators have had to refine their main message. The original wolf education message was something like, "Wolves are wonderful animals that have been misunderstood." The new message emphasized that wolves are wonderful when they live in wild places, but wolves living near people can be seriously troublesome. For this reason, some wolf advocates and groups have included a new mission, advocating for wild lands. With their long legs and wild hearts, wolves are poorly fit for life in tiny patches of habitat in a settled world. They do not do well when living cheek-by-jowl with humans. Wolves can only live like wolves if they are given enough room in which to live.

Wolves are messy, rough, and incorrigible. In the wilderness, that is no problem. It's a dog-eat-dog (or wolf-eat-deer) world out there, and wolves are supremely at home in such a setting. In semisettled lands where small blocks of brushy habitat are surrounded by farms, wolves – sooner or later – are likely to attack an animal prized by humans. A friend who worked tirelessly for wolf restoration once reflected, "This is not a warm and fuzzy critter. I love 'em, God knows I do, but the wolf is one hell-raising animal!"

Pendulum swings of opinion

Veteran wolf researchers have witnessed great swings in opinions about wolves in other societies. At various times and places, wolves have been tolerated or at least grudgingly accepted. They have often worn out their welcome, usually because they attacked livestock. That sparked retaliation in the form of harsh wolf control.

But then people often became uncomfortable with repressive wolf management, and so wolf policies shifted in favor of wolves. Wolves, with their great resiliency, have typically recovered quickly when not subjected to ferocious pressure. And then things have gone well . . . until a new surge in depredation caused people to sour on wolves again. In recent years, Poland has lurched through three of these great swings of attitudes toward wolves.

Veteran wolf researchers, managers, and educators worry about this. They believe these extreme oscillations in public wolf attitudes threaten the long-range future of wolves. The wisest wolf advocates I know believe in managing wolves in such a way as to reduce these great swings of popularity.

At this moment, I fear many wolf advocates hold an overly sanguine view of the potential for wolves to raise hell when they live in settled areas. We have just experienced several successful wolf restorations. The early years of wolf restoration are a sort of honeymoon period. Early in the restoration process, wolves occupy the best habitat, avoiding humans and eating wild game.

Trouble starts when the best habitat becomes saturated and wolves begin dispersing into marginal habitat closer to people. Dispersers are young, inexperienced wolves. When they set up territories in lands where there is little wild prey but an abundance of lambs, springer spaniels, turkeys, ponies, and other animals valued by humans, trouble seems almost inevitable.

Something like this might be happening in Wisconsin. The state's wolves rarely did anything to get in the newspapers in the early days of the restoration program. As their numbers built, Wisconsin wolves mostly minded their own business, although a few bear hunters lost hounds that were unlucky enough to dash into territory defended by a resident pack. In recent years, however, residents of northern counties

For wolves to live as wolves without getting in trouble with humans, they must have large blocks of habitat.

are complaining that wolf attacks on livestock and pets have become unacceptable.

This needs to be put in context. There are many farms in wolf country in Wisconsin. Although depredation is more common, the number of farms suffering attacks is still small as a percentage of the farms at risk. And it is still true that man's best friend, the dog, attacks more livestock each year than wolves. Even so, the losses are real. If you are the owner of a collie or a 4-H Charolais calf torn apart by wolves, you feel aggrieved.

Wolf managers in northern areas of the three states around Lake Superior have recently told me that the image of wolves might be changing in a negative direction. Great Lakes states managers used to confront wolf hatred based on myths and groundless fears. Now they face angry people who have suffered real harm from wolves.

Managing a hell-raising animal

What sort of management will reduce the swings in public attitudes toward wolves?

Four general management programs offer the most hope.

To ensure a future for wolves, we will need more and better wolf education. Wolf educators have debunked the silliest arguments put forward by those who hate wolves, and yet their task is far from done. Stupid hostile stereotypes about wolves are being replaced by stupid sentimental stereotypes, and both are dangerous.

Wolf educators need to exercise care and balance as they teach people about wolves. Mocking "Little Red Riding Hood" might still be useful for some audiences, but it is becoming necessary to admit that wolves can cause trouble when they live too near people. Wolf educators also need to teach livestock producers how to minimize wolf depredation.

Another necessary policy is zoning. Zoning simply means encouraging wolf populations in those places where wolves have a good chance to live like wolves without getting in trouble. Zoning also involves discouraging wolf populations in areas where conflict with humans is highly likely. Many wolf management plans include some sort of zoning.

Oddly enough, zoning is seen as "anti-wolf" by some wolf advocacy groups. They apparently believe that more wolves are better than few wolves, and they seem to expect that wolves will be able to live as model citizens in suburbs or little farm woodlots. I salute their faith in wolves, but find it naïve.

A third requirement is a strong wolf depredation control program. Such a program has to include two measures. People who lose pets or livestock to wolves deserve reasonable compensation.

As a society, we have chosen to bring wolves back. When wolves transgress, we should not expect a few individuals to bear the whole cost for a communal decision to include wild wolves in the modern world. A second necessary aspect of a depredation program is a program to quickly remove wolves that habitually get in trouble. Unhappily, that almost always means killing those wolves.

This, again, is seen as "anti-wolf" by many wolf fans. On the other hand, those managers who actually do the dirty work of killing depredating wolves always report that they love and admire wolves. They kill wolves that acquire the habit of attacking livestock or pets because they want to support society's desire to have wolves present. The wisest, most experienced managers I have met all agree that it isn't possible to have wolves in modern society without arrangements that promptly remove those

Without the ESA, it would not have been possible to restore an unpopular species like the wolf, given its troubled history. We cannot allow the ESA to be eviscerated now.

wolves that habitually prey on livestock or pets.

Finally, we should do everything possible to increase the number and size of wild lands where wolves can live freely as wolves. One form that might take is clustering smaller blocks of wild lands to form larger, contiguous lands. Some visionary environmentalists have talked about establishing a great wolf habitat corridor running the length of the Rocky Mountains. That would give wolves a wonderful great block of habitat. Every effort should be made to aggregate small blocks of habitat into larger blocks where wolves can be wolves.

Wolves are thriving now. Their future prospects are threatened by habitat fragmentation and global warming.

The ESA

Any discussion of the future of wolves must reflect on the law that has done so much for wolves. The ESA is the jewel in the crown of wildlife legislation. Its future is crucial for securing a future for wolves.

That means two things at least.

First, we need to defend the ESA by making sure that it works as it was intended to. The purpose of the ESA is to save species from extinction. Once saved, a formerly endangered species should be removed from the list. The whole point of the ESA is to take decisive action and then move on to save other species that are in peril (and alas, there is no shortage of them). It isn't a proper use of the ESA to park some species on the list in perpetuity. Similarly, it is dangerous to use the power of the ESA for other purposes – even good purposes, such as stopping unwise development. Because the ESA is so powerful, environmental groups are tempted to use it as an all-purpose weapon.

Some wolf fans are doing everything possible to keep the wolf on the endangered species list. They oppose delisting for what they regard as good motives. After all, wolves suffered under state management and thrived under federal protection. Some wolf advocates oppose delisting because they fear it will halt wolf restoration before enough wolves have been returned to enough suitable habitat.

Opposing delisting in areas where wolves have been successfully restored – as they have been in the western Great Lakes region and in the northern Rockies – seems shortsighted. People who hate the ESA often argue that the law is intrusive, rigid, and ineffective. One way to silence them would be to demonstrate the effectiveness of the act by making it work as it was intended. The return of wolves is one of the most magnificent accomplishments of modern game management. It is time to celebrate that victory by returning custody of wolves to states with sound wolf management plans.

Wolf advocates are having trouble accepting the new reality, which is that wolves are no longer "endangered" in any biological or political sense. Most state programs for managing wolves contain provisions for a hunting and/or trapping season, as this is the traditional way managers control wildlife populations. To many wolf advocates, this is abhorrent, for it allows private citizens to kill wolves. Some wolf fans do not trust state managers or private citizens to kill wolves without killing too many. Wolf advocates frequently doubt the judgment of wolf researchers and managers who assure them that wolves will do well under management protocols that include a public harvest.

Wolves are not going to become endangered again soon in North America. The ESA contains ample safeguards to prevent imperiled species from returning to endangered status after being listed and rescued. Beyond that, the whole climate of opinion on wolves has been transformed. A society that feared and hated wolves now appreciates them and wants to have them present in wild habitat. Wolf fans should welcome the coming of this new day instead of remaining locked in a mindset that confuses any wolf-killing with old wolf extirpation programs.

The second great requirement is to defend the ESA itself. I fear that many environmentalists are deluded about the security of that act. It has many powerful enemies. The ESA was adopted in a vastly different political climate than the one prevailing today. At that time, the two large national political parties were committed to environmental values. Now, only one is. I don't think there is a chance today's legislators would pass a law as robust and beneficial as the ESA. We should never take the existence of the ESA for granted.

It would probably be too risky for modern politicians to seek the outright repeal of the ESA, and yet the act could be sabotaged with far less dramatic changes. The ESA's opponents could pass an amendment requiring federal managers to consider possible negative economic impacts of any action they intend to take. That would gut the ESA. This act must be defended. It performs a crucial function and still has unique power. It absolutely must not be lost.

The maturation of a movement

I see the wolf restoration movement at a crossroads. The good news is that the movement has been a great success. While difficult local issues remain, wolf restoration has largely accomplished its goals. Wolves are now accepted as legitimate members of ecosystems in societies all the way from the Arctic to the US border with Mexico.

What is in doubt now is how wisely wolves will be managed in areas where people have gone to so much trouble to bring them back. The answer to that question might depend on how well the wolf restoration movement matures, by which I mean how well it adapts to new realities. Wolves have shown amazing ability to adapt to new realities. I wish the same were true for wolf people.

If wolf advocates continue to fight the old battle – poking fun at "The Three Little Pigs" and viewing any wolf killing as the unjustifiable sacrifice of an endangered animal – darker days might be ahead for wolves. If wolf fans continue to oppose any plans for a public harvest of wolves, if they oppose zoning, or if they fight reasonable depredation control efforts, the general good will that exists for wolves now could dissipate or disappear.

The most thoughtful, experienced, and committed wolf experts I know agree that wolves have their best chance for a good future if wolf fans accept management protocols that minimize wolf-human conflict. This will be difficult for some fans of wolves to accept, as any harsh treatment of individual wolves is abhorrent to people who have learned to love them. I understand that.

If wolf fans continue to press for more and more wolves in more and more places outside good wolf habitat, the result will be soaring depredation rates, and then the current public tolerance for wolves will be severely tested. To be sure, if there is a return in local areas to harsh wolf control, that will not be fatal to wolves. Wolves are resilient and we have learned too much about the positive side of wolves to ever go back to 14th-century attitudes toward them. But the most desirable outcome for wolves depends on wolf fans accepting sound management programs designed to allow people and wolves to coexist with no more violence on either side than is absolutely necessary.

Wolf restoration has involved a rough bargain. In crude terms, advocates have told opponents, "Let us have wolves, and we will direct managers to remove the ones that offend." That wasn't a deal that wolf opponents wanted to accept because they would be the ones living near wolves and thus had most to lose, but they generally lost the argument. It seems only fair now for wolf advocates to keep our side of the bargain. Although it might seem contradictory, the future of wolves will be enhanced if wolf advocates agree to management that promptly removes wolves that habitually get in trouble.

This adjustment will be challenging for wolf advocacy groups. The surest way for wolf organizations to gain new members and encourage existing members to contribute checks is to portray wolves as victims. It isn't cynical to note a simple truth: wolf groups are severely tempted to dramatize harsh treatment of wolves, portraying it as old-fashioned wolf hatred. Because wolf groups are passionately committed to do well by wolves, they find it difficult to avoid the emotional fundraising pitches that they know work best for them.

In this context, special praise is owed the International Wolf Center (IWC). The IWC has dedicated itself to educating people about wolves with information that is balanced and scientifically valid. Visitors have been surprised to learn that the IWC is not a wolf advocacy group in the usual sense. The IWC, for example, doesn't hesitate to talk about wolf depredation, although it is enthusiastic in its support of wolves worldwide. IWC mailings do not feature bloody photos of "slaughtered" wolves or talk hysterically about the "plight" of some threatened wolf pack. Projecting a sober, balanced view of wolves has meant bypassing a great deal of potential support from people who respond compassionately to emotional pitches. Wolf fans should support wolf groups that promote mature and balanced views of wolves.

To win a place for wolves in the modern world it has been necessary to have the earnest efforts of all sorts of wolf groups. Now it might be time for wolf advocates to restrain emotional arguments and support wolf management that has the best chance to secure a place for wolves in the future. Wolf advocates have to acknowledge the reasonable concerns of people who live near wolves and who occasionally pay a price for our societal decision to include wolves in modern ecosystems.

In the distant future

In the short term, prospects for wolves look excellent. They won't be "everywhere" they used to be, but wolves will clearly be a significant presence in major areas of the North American continent for the next few decades.

I'm less optimistic about the distant future. There are at least two major trends threatening the future of wolves.

First is the continued upward trend of human populations, along with the inevitable loss of habitat to development that comes with it. When people build cabins in forested areas, wolves lose habitat. When roads are blazed through state forests, wolves lose habitat. When people upgrade highways so vehicles can travel at higher speeds in wolf country, wolves lose. The process is insidious because it happens in such small increments, like water dripping on a stone.

I don't see a way to stop or reverse that trend. Human populations are going up. People are infiltrating wild lands because those places are beautiful places to erect a home or recreational home. Wherever people go, they bring their dogs and all the diseases those dogs carry, and that is bad for wolves. All of this is slowly reducing wolf habitat to smaller and increasingly isolated patches.

The second trend is global warming. While some people choose to believe that global warming is a controversial theory, the vast majority of scientists agree that human activity is turning up the temperature of the planet. If global warming continues at the current pace, at some point we will be nostalgic for the time when it seemed worthwhile to fight about such a romantic topic as wolves.

The return of the wolf represents man's triumph over some of his own worst qualities. It is cause for hope.

A second chance

While my work on this book has convinced me it is foolish to reduce wolves to symbols, I believe the restoration of wolves will be a major event in human history. Humans in general – and North Americans in particular – have abused wolves. We owe it to the wolf to try one more time to work out a relationship that protects legitimate human interests while allowing wolves a reasonable amount of living space.

Further, I would argue, we owe it to ourselves to try again to manage wolves wisely. When the residents of the US and Canada finally learn to tolerate and respect wolves, we will have exorcised something singularly ugly from our national characters.

While I believe wolf restoration is going to proceed successfully in many regions, I don't expect it to be easy. Greed, fear, and other deep-seated human traits will continue to complicate our relationship with wolves.

And wolves themselves will keep the process difficult. Wolves are smart, tough, and resourceful. Wolves that live near people are always a threat to attack livestock or pets. With their great fertility, wolves are capable of expanding their populations rapidly. Another difficulty of managing wolves is their great mobility. Most wild animals restrict their activities to a small geographic area, but wolves are apt to take off and move hundreds of miles in a few days. When wolves learn to go after livestock, they can be incorrigible.

A crucial issue is whether wolves might lose their fear of humans. At the time I wrote the first edition of this book, wolf authorities assured me that wolves were "shy" and naturally afraid of humans. Since then, there have been several documented instances of wolves becoming habituated to people. Wolves learned to beg for food in Algonquin Park and on a British Columbian island frequented by kayakers. The wolves of Denali Park and Yellowstone Park routinely conduct daily activities near spectators, paying them no attention. When people quit being a threat to wolves, wolves are smart enough to recognize that fact. Fear of people is not in their genes, but in their heads. Wolves that become too comfortable around people are more of a threat than fans of wolves might like to believe.

It might be part of the long, tragic history of humans and wolves that the only way we can live near them is by being aggressive toward them. This is not a position I enjoy adopting. Obviously, we do not need to abuse wolves as people historically have. Yet it seems likely that humans will need to harass or even hunt wolves to keep them wary of us.

The true measure of the morality of a political society is how justly it treats its least powerful and popular citizens. In much the same sense, the ecological decency of a society can be measured by how it treats the most troublesome and notorious animal species. For our society, that is the wolf.

When North Americans prove we have learned to live with wolves, we can begin to like ourselves a little better. It will then be time to ponder how we can improve our relations with several hundred other species, but not before pausing to celebrate the extraordinary progress represented by the return of the wolf.

About the Author and the Main Photographer

Steve Grooms has been studying and writing about wolves since 1977. His early background includes a Masters degree in American Studies and work as a college administrator, writing instructor, and freelance outdoor writer and photographer. From 1976 through 1981 he was managing editor of *Fins and Feathers Magazine*. In that role, he wrote what was probably the first sporting magazine's endorsement of wolf restoration programs.

Since 1981 Steve has been writing books and articles on his own. He is the author of 13 books on a wide range of subjects he finds fascinating: pheasant hunting, outdoor philosophy and humor, natural history, fishing and fishing boats, trophy deer, health, cooking — even a memoir.

Earlier editions of *Return of the Wolf* won the Skipping Stones Prize (2000) and earned an endorsement from the National Wildlife Federation. The book appeals to the general public but also has been used as a textbook. Not surprisingly, Steve is a member of the International Wolf Center and serves on the Center's the magazine committee.

Steve lives in St. Paul, Minnesota and has sighted five Wisconsin wolves on the way to his cabin near Cornucopia.

Michael H. Francis, trained as a wildlife biologist, is a wildlife photographer based in Montana. His photography has been internationally recognized for its beautiful and informative imagery. Mike's work has been published by the National Geographic Society, The Audubon Society, The National Wildlife Federation; as well as by *Field & Stream*, *Outdoor Life*, and *Sports Afield* magazines, among others.

Mike's contributions to this book come from his archive of more than 8,400 wolf images, many of which were shot in the wild. He is the sole photographer for 26 books. Mike is the past president of the North American Nature Photography Association. Mike lives in Billings, Montana with his wife, two daughters, and 26 turtles and tortoises.

Publisher's note: It's common to see acknowledgements from authors that thank all the people who contribute to the work that finally appears, the a result of everyone's magnificent efforts. We would like to tweak that tradition and thank Steve and Mike for their extraordinary generosity, good will and uncompromising professionalism in making this third edition of *Return of the Wolf* a pleasure to work on and, we hope, a treasure for readers.

Index

Maps are indicated by **boldface** type.